The Deaf Jew
in the Modern World

The Deaf Jew
in the Modern World

Edited by
JEROME D. SCHEIN
and
LESTER J. WALDMAN

KTAV PUBLISHING HOUSE, INC.
for
NEW YORK SOCIETY FOR THE DEAF
1986

Library of Congress Cataloging-in-Publication Data
Main entry under title:

The Deaf Jew in the modern world.

L. Jewish way of life—Addresses, essays, lectures.
2. Deaf—Religious life—Addresses, essays, lectures.
I. Schein, Jerome Daniel.   II. Waldman, Lester J.
III. Title.
BM700.D44   1985   296'.08808162   85-24218
ISBN 0-88125-096-1

MANUFACTURED IN THE UNITED STATES OF AMERICA

Dedication

It is extremely fitting that this volume be a memorial to Fred Milfred. It was his colleagues in the New York Society for the Deaf and other friends whose generosity made possible the conference at which many of the following papers were presented. From that conference grew the idea of a publication to further the impetus gained from that meeting toward encouraging a broader discussion of the problems confronting Jewish deaf people.

Fred Milfred, a graduate of New York University, was a businessman who believed that his business included his efforts to improve the condition of his fellow men and women. When he died, in July 1979, he had served as president of New York Lodge No. 1 of B'nai Brith, as a trustee and as president of Temple Israel of New York, and as a vigorous defender of human rights by his leadership roles in the Anti-Defamation League.

Fred had a great interest in deaf people. For more than fifteen years he was a member of the board of directors of the New York Society for the Deaf and for three years its vice-president. He gave both his time and his resources to further the work of the society.

It has been said that how a man used his days tells us who he was. By that standard, Fred Milfred left a rich harvest of service to others. It is that record, in addition to this volume, which is his true memorial.

Hon. Joseph G. Blum
Chairman of the Board
New York Society for the Deaf

Contents

Acknowledgments

This monograph grew out of a conference of the same name, which was held 10 November 1981 in New York City. The society's religious committee—Bernard Brownstein, John L. Goldwater, Milton Ohringer, with Harold R. Shapiro, chair, and Rabbi Ronald B. Sobel, as co-chair—guided the development of the conference and assisted ably in conducting it.

The material in Appendix A regarding the attitude to the deaf of Jewish law was made available to us by Bar Ilan University, for which we thank them.

The conference honored the memory of the late Fred B. Milfred, a member of the board of the New York Society for the Deaf, who had shown, throughout his life, great compassion for his fellow humans in general, and for deaf people in particular. Funds contributed in his memory have been used to develop this publication.

Another deceased member of the board of the New York Society for the Deaf, David Litter, provided further impetus toward publicizing the problems of Jewish deaf people, as well as additional funds for doing so, by his gift with which to assist in the distribution of information about deafness.

Other individuals and organizations who have contributed to the printing and distribution of this volume are the Federation of Jewish Philanthropies of Greater New York City, Bernard Brownstein, and John Goldwater, former president of the New York

Society for the Deaf and presently a member of its board, who provided special publication funds.

To all of the above, the New York Society for the Deaf expresses its deep gratitude for affording it the opportunity to continue its long-standing efforts to meet the social, vocational, and religious needs of deaf people. Coming as it does in the year of the society's seventy-fifth anniversary, this publication provides additional evidence of the society's commitment to serve the deaf community.

Introduction

Under talmudic law, a deaf person who did not speak could not assume full citizenship in the Jewish community. A born-deaf male could not be counted in establishing a minyan, nor could he enter into contracts. These strictures were not meant to be cruel but were seen as the means of protecting such individuals from exploitation by others, while recognizing that they could not contribute fully to the religious life of the community. Those proscriptions, laid down almost two millennia ago, did not anticipate the advent of electronic hearing aids nor the advances in the education of deaf children. The very meaning of the word *deaf* must be reconsidered in the light of technological progress and educational changes that greatly alter its earlier connotations.

The question arises, then, What is the position of the deaf Jew in the modern world?

Deafness Redefined

Deafness cannot be understood in its human terms without consideration of two aspects: the degree of hearing impairment and the age of the individual at its onset. As Professor Maurice Miller points out in his essay, humans can hear sounds ranging from very low frequencies, like the bass notes on a piano, to very high frequencies, like the treble notes of a piccolo. But most important to humans are the middle-range frequencies— the sounds of speech. When the degree of impairment pre-

1

vents a person from hearing and understanding speech, that person is *deaf*. That is the meaning that is used in the following chapters. All other connotations of the word notwithstanding, deafness refers to the inability to carry on a conversation with eyes closed. This definition takes account of lipreading, a talent some people develop to overcome their loss of hearing. While not specifying any audiometric levels, the statement makes clear that our concern with deafness is for its disruption of communication. That is the vital, the devastating, consequence of deafness.

But knowing how much, or how little, a person hears will not complete our account of the likely effects of deafness. A second factor is the individual's age at its onset. Deafness at birth or before the development of speech—prelingual deafness—will interfere with communication in ways that deafness occurring in adulthood does not. Prelingually deaf persons have great difficulty in developing speech, if they learn to speak at all, and their grasp of language is severely impaired. They grow up dependent on vision for communication, usually preferring to communicate manually rather than orally. Those deafened in childhood also have impaired speech and language, though to a lesser degree. With modern amplification and educational techniques, the impact of deafness on speech and language is being lessened, but for deaf adults, living today, who did not have the benefits of such intervention, the reality is that they are communicatively handicapped.

Deafness occurring in adulthood, on the other hand, does not regressively interfere with speech and language when both are already fully developed. Adult deafness presents other problems, problems associated with the emotional and economic consequences of being unable freely to communicate.

As the first essay, by Rabbi Feldman, makes clear, the talmudic injunctions concerning deafness were directed at prelingually deaf persons, not those who lost hearing in adulthood. This monograph, therefore, will focus on early deafness.

In all of the following pages, then, when the word *deaf* is used without further specification, it refers only to people deafened in childhood or early adolescence.

The Deaf Community

Deaf people share speech and language disabilities. They also share a little-known culture: motivated by their common interests, the majority of early-deafened people tend to associate with each other. Whether because they find it easier to mingle with other deaf people or because they are frequently rejected by those who find it difficult to communicate with them, early-deafened people have created a world of their own—the Deaf Community.

The Deaf Community exists alongside of the general communities in which it is embedded. It has all the hallmarks of a community: organizations of, not for, deaf people at local, state, regional, and national levels. The National Association of the Deaf, probably the first nationwide organization of a disabled group, was founded in 1880. Its members reside in every state of the United States. In turn, NAD has affiliated state associations, and many of these have affiliates in the major cities. Other national organizations, like the American Athletic Association of the Deaf, represent particular interests within the Deaf Community. The National Congress of the Jewish Deaf, for instance, is but one of several groups of deaf coreligionists.

The Deaf Community has also established institutions to serve its economic needs. The National Fraternal Society of the Deaf is one of this country's most successful insurance companies. Founded at the turn of the century, when deaf people were often rejected for life insurance, NFSD has grown to provide insurance not only to deaf people in the United States but also in Canada. In addition to providing life insurance for its members, NFSD also offers charitable and community services, such as providing scholarships for young deaf people. At the local level, agencies like the Greater Los Angeles Council on Deafness (known as GLAD) provide a wide range of social and rehabilitative services to deaf persons in their areas; GLAD, for instance, operates a book store and lobbies for deaf causes.

The reality of the Deaf Community is represented in the extensive communication network that it supports. Newspapers and magazines, some local and some national, report on events of interest to deaf people—much as the media for any group. Efforts to sponsor television broadcasts in sign language have been less successful, but no less revealing of the strong feelings of community among the majority of deaf people.

The cement that binds the Deaf Community of the United States is American Sign Language. It is preferred by deaf persons because it is adapted to the eye, just as English is adapted to the ear. However, ASL is not a version of English conveyed by hand signals. ASL has its own vocabulary and its own syntax. For the majority of deaf persons in the United States, English is a second language. This point needs to be borne in mind when communicating with ASL-fluent deaf persons. Their odd expressions in English illustrate no lack of intelligence. Like foreign-born persons, many deaf persons use English imperfectly because it has been taught imperfectly. They lack the practice leading to overlearning that comes from constant use of a language. But these same deaf people are usually fluent in ASL, their "native" language (or more correctly, the language which they practice most).[1]

This brief description of a cultural phenomenon cannot convey the richness of the social lives of most deaf people. Certainly, they lack ease of communication with the population at large. They suffer from discrimination of many kinds, none of it pleasant and much of it economically harmful. However, deaf people in the United States have been fiercely independent. In 1947, the president of NAD appeared before the

United States Congress and urged it *not* to provide an extra income-tax exemption for deaf persons! Instead, he asked Congress to support education for deaf children, because then, he said, they could compete equally with their fellow citizens. The income-tax exemption would only set them further apart from the general population. Not all NAD members agreed with that sentiment, especially since blind people are granted an extra exemption. Not all deaf persons desire, nor are all capable of, independence. Still, the action of the highest official elected solely by deaf people exemplifies the efforts they have made to be free to manage their own lives in their own ways.

Most deaf people—those who have created and who sustain the Deaf Community—have earned their neighbors' respect, though seldom have they had their understanding. It is to this lack of understanding that the present monograph has been addressed. It seeks to broaden the public's appreciation of deaf people and their problems. Especially, it hopes to acquaint the hearing members of the Jewish community with their deaf coreligionists.

Background of the Monograph

The New York Society for the Deaf has felt a responsibility to open this issue to the considered judgment of the Jewish community, as well as to provide deaf Jews with an opportunity to ventilate their opinions. The society's board recognized the organization's obligation both to its deaf constituency and to the Jewish community that provides a substantial portion of its support. In preparing this monograph, the editors have endeavored to introduce a number of viewpoints. Our intention is to educate, not to indoctrinate. We have not, however, included a statement by any group, if there is one, that holds the belief that deafness per se warrants exclusion from the houses of worship and from participation in the affairs of the religious community. Given the considerable advances in technology and the reinterpretations of sacred texts that occur from time to time in the dynamic Jewish culture, which in turn is embedded in our evolving modern society, the board of the New York Society for the Deaf voted to hold a conference on the deaf Jew in the modern world in November 1981.

No attempt has been made to produce a record of that conference as such. Rather, this monograph endeavors to capture the spirit of that meeting and to preserve the thoughtful expressions by the distinguished speakers whose presentations are reproduced. In some instances, the authors have elected to rewrite their speeches to better accommodate the print modality or to bring them up to date. The editors have added some material that they uncovered after the conference and felt was germane to the monograph. The order in which the articles appear differs from the order in which they were given at the conference. The revision reflects only the editors' attempts to present ideas to the readers in an attractive and informative manner. Nothing should be inferred as to the value of the articles from their priority within this monograph.

The Contents

The essays that make up this volume represent the experiences of several deaf leaders and several rabbis, as well as the opinions of some practitioners with a professional interest in hearing impairment and its attendant social-psychological problems. In preparing this monograph for publication, we have had an excellent opportunity to reflect upon what has been learned from this review of an ancient tradition as it confronts the changes brought about by science and social evolution.

Rabbi Feldman's brilliant exegesis of the talmudic views of early deafness displays not only great religious scholarship but also a depth of appreciation for the nuances of deafness in its various forms. He concludes his remarkably laconic historical review by laying the foundation for a change in those earlier views—a change based upon a reinterpretation of what deafness means. To further make comprehensible points raised by Rabbi Feldman, selected quotations from the Talmud and the Responsa are reproduced in Appendix A.

The sermon by Rabbi Adler, written in 1864, makes clear that the problems of and interest in deaf Jews are not being confronted for the first time here. This century-old article stands in contrast to the recent paper presented by the Ashkenazi chief rabbi of Israel, Shlomo Goren. The contrast between it and Rabbi Adler's thoughts reflects the semantic restructuring recommended by Rabbi Feldman. The three papers, taken together with the later chapters by Rabbis Goldstein and Grossman, illustrate the adaptation of religious views to social-technical progress.

Deaf Jews have not always accepted without protest their exclusion from religious life, as witness the chapters written by Drs. Frederick C. Schreiber and T. Alan Hurwitz, Alexander Fleischman, and Meyer Lief. Unfortunately, the views of these four deaf leaders have not had wide circulation outside of the Deaf Community. The late Dr. Frederick C. Schreiber was executive secretary of the National Association of the Deaf when he made the address on which his chapter is based. Founded in 1880, NAD was the first nationwide organization *of* disabled people. It is a self-help group, not an organization of able-bodied people trying to aid physically disabled persons. As the leader of that organization, Dr. Schreiber often expressed his opinions on the major issues facing his constituents. He spoke eloquently about what it means to be a deaf Jew, and his words carry the authority of his national position.

Additional expressions by two current national deaf leaders, Hurwitz and Fleischman, expand Schreiber's thesis. Both hold elected offices that display the great esteem in which they are held by deaf people throughout the country. Indeed, Fleischman is president of the international organization of Jewish deaf people. The experiences of these two leaders and those of their deaf fellows make clear why shifts in attitudes toward today's well-educated, high-achieving deaf population are in order—not solely for the welfare of deaf people but also for the benefit of Jewish society, which misses much when it lacks the active participation of its deaf membership.

The paper by Meyer Lief, a revered elder member of the Hebrew Association of the Deaf, reminds us that efforts to educate young deaf Jews have been made for many years—by other deaf Jews. In reciting that historical anecdote, Mr. Lief indirectly highlights the neglect of many deaf adolescents' Jewish heritage. As Fleischman also points out, those young deaf people living in areas less densely populated than cities like New York have attended schools and played after hours with few, if any, other Jewish children. They grew up without an opportunity to know their own religion.

That inroads on past attitudes have been made and are continuing to be made with exceptional vigor is demonstrated in the papers by Rabbis Elyse Goldstein and Daniel Grossman. Their chapters discuss religious services with deaf congregants and the efforts to overcome the language barriers. The deaf congregation cannot appreciate the sound of Hebrew, nor can its members understand, without interpretation, the English that may be spoken in a service. Lipreading, while inexact at best, becomes impossible at distances beyond 20 to 30 feet for persons with normal vision. Sign language, on the other hand, can be comprehended at distances of 100 feet or more—visually ample for most auditoriums. Rabbis Goldstein and Grossman, along with their discussions of other aspects of meeting the religious needs of deaf Jews, present some of the adaptations that have been made to ASL to manage the liturgy. As has been demonstrated in countless other situations, any concept that can be transmitted by speech can be signed. The prayer book reproduced as Appendix B reinforces the point, again, that efforts to serve the religious needs of deaf Jews are not new. Almost seventy years old, the book simplified the language used, in order to make it more readable for deaf people who had difficulty reading English. Whether the effort was or was not misguided, it revealed a welcome desire to accommodate religious materials for a neglected part of the congregation.

The problems of deafness are exacerbated by old age. Adjustments carefully honed over the years become inadequate for many deaf people as they enter senescence. Reduced vigor, impairment of vision, loss of income, changes in social relations—these and many other problems confront the elderly deaf person. Dr. Lester J. Waldman has served the Deaf Community for many years, as a member of the board, President, executive director, and presently counsel to the board of the New York Society for the Deaf. The richness of his experience qualifies him to point to the glaring shortcomings in the services being provided deaf persons. He discusses the special difficulties facing aging deaf persons. In the course of his presentation, he recommends corrective measures, some of which are already being taken by NYSD in response to his promptings, and all of which are worthy of implementing.

The internationally acclaimed audiologist, Dr. Maurice Miller, succinctly introduces critical scientific advances in modern-day views of deafness. His remarks provide another valuable context from which to ponder the issues raised in the different intellectual settings of the other chapters. In particular, he makes clear the relations between the growth of our understanding of the hearing process and the inventions that now make possible remediation of disorders of that process.

A final chapter endeavors to put the discussions of deafness and religion in a broader perspective, reviewing the scanty demographic evidence on the religious preferences of and participation by deaf persons, and considering the provisions made by various religious groups for those members of their congregations who are deaf. This chapter implies nothing with respect to which religion is best for deaf people; such judgments are left to individual consciences. What the chapter strives to do is to reveal the varieties of actions and reactions, by deaf people and by religious organizations, in order to facilitate the consideration by religious leaders of what they might, or might not, wish to do about their deaf constituents.

Some Concluding Words

The question that has directed the compilation of this monograph is: What is the position of the deaf Jew in the modern world? That empirical question precedes moral questions; it asks *what* and not *should*. Furthermore, it asks what is the *current* standing of deaf Jews, though recognizing that the present cannot be understood without a knowledge of the past.

To answer the principal question, the editors have selected a distinguished group of authors and some cogent examples from other times. The chosen essayists have not been bound by any limitations on their views. In discussing the topic of this monograph, they have ranged widely, providing much information and many opinions.

In setting forth the great variety of opinions and experiences represented in the following chapters, the editors have striven to reflect accurately what the authors intended. We have had the invaluable assistance of Rabbi Mark Hurvitz, who joined the New York Society for the Deaf's staff only two years ago and who also serves as the religious leader of the Hebrew Association of the Deaf. Despite his brief association with deaf people, Rabbi Hurvitz has already become a proficient manual communicator and their warm supporter. He has been unusually generous with his precious few free hours. If there are errors in transcription of the manuscripts, however, the fault lies with the editors, not with Rabbi Hurvitz nor with the authors.

At the conference from which most of these papers were drawn, Rabbi Ronald B. Sobel delivered the benediction. He has for many years served as a member of the board and, as at present, as an honorary director of the New York Society for the Deaf. His knowledge of deaf people and his position as one of the foremost Jewish religious leaders in the United States gave special congency to his summation. Reviewing the preceding addresses and the lively discussion they stimulated, Rabbi Sobel extracted a beautiful message: "What these deliberations have provided is an exercise in love."

In the spirit generated by those words, the New York Society for the Deaf has striven to bring the position of the deaf Jew to wide attention, confident that people of goodwill can find and will adopt the right course of action for the future. If the reader leaves these collected papers with fresh insights and encouragement to accept the challenge that new knowledge brings, then the society's mission will be fulfilled, and the credit will clearly belong to the distinguished authors who have sacrificed their time to share their wisdom on behalf of their fellows.

Note
1. For a fuller discussion of sign languages and their role in the Deaf Community, see J. D. Schein, *Speaking the Language of Sign* (New York: Doubleday, 1984).

Deafness and Jewish Law and Tradition

Rabbi David M. Feldman

The situation of the deaf Jew begins with a very negative principle in Jewish law. This is the talmudic phrase which combines and compares the *ḥeresh* with the *shoteh* and *katan*.

In all cases of marriage and divorce, of making contracts, of the buying of movable and immovable property, the Talmud says there are three categories of people that cannot engage in these activities. The three categories of people who cannot perform these legal acts, nor participate in many of the rituals of Jewish life, are the *ḥeresh*, *shoteh*, and *katan*. They are the deaf-mute, the lunatic, and the minor. These three categories are grouped together because of the assumed common limitations in their ability to communicate and be communicated with, and therefore to understand what they are doing. They are therefore severely limited and restricted from participating in the above-mentioned activities. This is the stark negative statement received from the tradition. Unfortunately the phrase remains in the back of the mind of so many. *Ḥeresh, shoteh, katan,* lumping together these three categories.

A distinguished Jewish scholar who graduated from Yeshiva University and the Jewish Theological Seminary, which granted him his ordination, Rabbi Feldman is the author of *Abortion and Jewish Law*. He serves as co-chair of the Medical Ethics Committee of the Federation of Jewish Philanthropies and is the spiritual leader of the Jewish Community Center, Teaneck, New Jersey.

However, in the development of the Talmud and Jewish law up until this day, there is a series of qualifying clauses of improvements and refinements. In fact, the concept of *ḥeresh* has been well-nigh removed from the bad company in which the original mishnaic formulation of the Talmud had placed it.

When the Mishnah says *ḥeresh*, the Talmud declares that it does not mean a deaf person only, it means the deaf-mute; it means one who can neither hear *nor* speak. One who cannot hear or speak, it is presumed, has been denied the ability to communicate properly. If a person cannot communicate or be communicated with, then it must be assumed that he cannot learn what things are all about. Therefore, his *kavvanah* (intent) to marry, to divorce, to buy, to sell, to give *ḥalitzah* (in the levirate ritual), to put on tefillin or to perform other ritual observances—let alone the social deeds and activities he might engage in, if they have legal context to them—is inadequate. We must assume he cannot do them if he cannot hear or speak. But if he can speak, then of course he can communicate even though he cannot hear. Because if he can speak, then he can say what he wants to know, and then the others can make these things known to him, knowing what he has said. And so one giant step forward has been taken by saying that as long as a person can speak, the loss of hearing alone no longer remains a disqualifying disability.

By virtue of his ability to communicate through speaking, he is able to remove from himself the total restriction and total disqualification of the Mishnah. Once he can communicate he is able to understand and do much more.

There are, however, halachic authorities who say that being able to communicate through speech is still not enough to free a deaf person from certain restrictions. Maimonides maintained that a person who can speak but not hear can engage in marriage or divorce or other ritual activities. But when it comes to buying or selling property, Maimonides felt that there may be a lot that the deaf person is missing by virtue of the fact that he cannot hear. Thus he suggests that perhaps we ought to preclude him from the possibility of buying and selling because he might be misled by what he cannot hear—things said behind his back. Therefore, even though he can speak, the fact that he cannot hear would seem to disqualify him from selling or buying of properties. The consequences of these acts are long-range. Therefore Maimonides retains that disability, even for the deaf person who is not a deaf-mute.

Rabbi Abraham ben David, the Ravad, Maimonides' principal opponent, who dissents wherever there is room for debate, disagrees here as well. According to the Ravad, if the deaf person cannot hear but can speak, that is good enough. He can sell and buy properties because he can make himself heard; he can speak and say, "Tell me the real price, tell me whether this is really a good deal." As long as he can speak, the deaf person has no more disqualification even in matters pertaining to real property. That is a giant step.

The next major steps in the history of halachic development deal with the removal of other aspects of disqualification. What if one cannot hear or speak but can hear with the assistance of an ear-horn or a trumpet? These have been used for the past 250 years. Now they have been entirely superseded by mechanical hearing aides. Already in the nineteenth century the halachic authorities said that as long as a person can hear with assistance, he can hear. That is all that is necessary. Such a person is now *k'pikkeach l'khol davar*. He is as "open-minded" and as whole and functional as anyone else. The Halachah states that there are no longer any disabilities so long as he can hear, even with assistance, such as the horn.

The far greater advance in neutralizing the legal disqualification is by considering the reason why the deaf-mute cannot engage in these activities. If the reason is that he cannot communicate and therefore remains unaware, then what if he goes to a school where he is taught a sign language or lipreading? Or is taught to communicate despite total disability of hearing and speaking? Then we must say that he is able to learn and to understand and to make himself as understood as those who have no impairment to begin with.

In the subsequent history of Jewish law, some rabbis accept this—let us call it—functional definition, others do not. To them, the principle of *ḥeresh* still remains, even if the person in question goes to school. He remains in the category of the restricted, and the category cannot be abolished. There is a small book from the nineteenth century, with articles by several rabbis, titled *Melechet Ḥeresh*, the "Work of the Deaf." Five of the rabbis represented in this book decided that a person who goes to a school for the deaf and learns to overcome his impairment by being able to communicate in other ways should have no more legal limitations placed upon him. Five others retained the category and the limitations.

Rabbi Hayim of Tsanz, the Tsanzer Rebbe, would not go that far. According to him, if the deaf person learned even to stammer a bit, he would be okay. But not even able to stammer—he would still be in the category of the deaf-mute. The deaf-mute who can communicate with sign language is not yet one who speaks. The others said that the fact that he can communicate with his hands, that he can communicate in any way, makes him as qualified and as unrestricted legally, as undisabled as all the rest of us.

In the summer of 1982, the World Congress of Jewish Deaf, Agudat Haḥareshim, met in convention in Israel. They were addressed by Rabbi Louis Rabinowitz, who was formerly chief rabbi of South Africa and at that time was deputy mayor of Jerusalem. He presented a very strong statement in which he claimed that the whole concept of joining *ḥeresh*, *shoteh*, and *katan* is bad. However, he said, it is also instructive. If you think more about the three categories that are refused participation in so many things, the *ḥeresh*, deaf-mute, the *shoteh*, or lunatic, and the *katan*, minor, you notice the structure of their differences. The difference between the lunatic and the minor is that a lunatic is and remains a lunatic (a *na'ar bleibt a na'ar*, as they say in Yiddish). But a *katan*, a minor, is remediable. As I say to many of the older people in my congregation, "Youth is a good thing, but youth is a curable disease." In other words you get over it. You get over youth (maybe too soon), but youth is a curable disease. Rabbi Rabinowitz said something similar to the Association of the Jewish Deaf. The *katan*, the minor in these three categorizations, is in a situation which corrects itself. The minor becomes Bar or Bat Mitzvah and then he or she is no longer a minor. So you have two categories which point in different directions. The *shoteh*, the lunatic, is presumably in a chronic permanent situation, while the *katan* is in a temporary correctible situation. This is as if to teach that there are two kinds of *heresh*. There is the permanent deaf-mute, the kind the Talmud would disqualify. But a *heresh* in the category of the minor, namely, one whose situation will be corrected either with time or with learning or with school—such a one is disqualified only temporarily, only until he is a *heresh shenitrappeh*, a deaf-mute who has now been "cured." Cured even partially, he is able to participate in all activities: rituals, contracts, marriage, divorce, etc.

What is interesting is that there seem to be ivory-tower people and then the practical rabbis. The ivory-tower people are the ones who take a text, and on the basis of the text they make their conclusions. The Tsanzer Rebbe, for example, and others more so, take this statement in the Mishnah about the *heresh* not being able to do certain things. They, like Maimonides, said that even if he can speak he cannot sell property, and they take that literally. They preserved a category. They also preserved the category with regard to other mitzvot, other rituals and obligations in Jewish law. They took this category and froze it at that level.

Even the first Lubavitcher Rebbe, the Tzemach Tzedeck, Rabbi Shneur Zalman, in the nineteenth century, said that the Talmud presents a category of a deaf-mute and it is unchangeable. The deaf-mute remains a category no matter what kind of training you are going to give him in communication. On the other hand, there is Rabbi Simcha Bunim Sofer, the grandson of the Hatam Sofer, the famous Moses Sofer, who died in 1839 in Hungary. This grandson said he understood Rabbi Schneur Zalman theoretically, but practically he had a different experience. He went to visit one of the schools where deaf-mutes were taught to communicate in sign language or through other means. He was greatly impressed, first by the modern techniques, secondly by the results achieved. Therefore, he disagreed with his great teacher the Tzemach Tzedeck and instead followed the teaching of his father. He would approve of his conclusion by virtue of having seen first-hand that we have here an entirely different situation. The schools for the training of the deaf are now so effective, so efficient, so competent, in both their means and their results, that he had to side with those who say we are dealing now with a whole different category. These students are no longer in the category of the deaf-mute. The talmudic idea no longer applies where we have removed the original problem, namely, their failure to communicate, which presumably implied their failure to understand, and therefore to contract. That is indeed a major step. This also throws light on the role of the subjective nature of the *posek*, the one who decides Jewish law. It proves once again that one must get out of the ivory tower and not make decisions on the basis of texts pored over in the closed study halls, but come out and see what life is really about.

Along the same lines Rabbi Isaac Herzog, who was chief rabbi of Israel until 1959, declared that those who remain in the ivory tower and say the schools are not good enough do not realize the techniques that have been developed in the schools. He goes on to describe the techniques used in the schools and suggests that once they are known, one's point of view must change. You have got to do so and then remove all limitations that still exist surrounding the technically deaf-mute.

Our subject is of interest from another standpoint. If we are not happy with the pace of development of Jewish law, with the history of the deaf's legal disabilities and their removal, there is the nonlegal side, the aggadic aspect. Here the attitude to the *ḥeresh* is so positive, so sympathetic. This, of course, presents a different kind of problem. The aggadic attitude is so positive, but that, to some, seems patronizing, condescending. If Jewish law is unsympathetic to the deaf, that would be terrible. But if it is sympathetic, it can seem patronizing, something that also violates respect for the self-sufficiency of the so-called disabled. Forgive, then, the apparently patronizing.

The positive attitude toward the deaf begins, of course, with the Bible. Leviticus 19:14, says: *"Lo t'kallel ḥeresh*—Thou shalt not curse the deaf."* What does this mean? On the face of it one would say, It is so obvious it would seem to be superfluous. As a matter of fact, the Talmud says so. How can anyone be so cruel as to curse the deaf?! How can anyone *need* to be told otherwise? Or, as the second half of the same verse says, "do not place a stumbling block before the blind." Also obvious. Who would be so cruel as to place a stumbling block before the blind?! The Torah need not rule on something so obviously forbidden, so obviously indecent. Therefore, says the Talmud, this cannot be meant literally. What it really means is, Don't curse a person who is able to hear you but who is *like* the deaf in that he was too far away to hear and respond. Don't curse a person who is not there to defend himself, is what it means. And "do not place a stumbling block before the blind" also must be taken figuratively. It means, Don't lead astray by exposing one to temptation. Not the literally blind, but those who are unable to see what you see. Other commentaries say that there is still much to be learned from this verse in its literal sense. You may think it okay to curse the deaf because the deaf cannot feel hurt, cannot get angry at you, not having heard what you said. You may curse them and they will still think that you like them, that you are still their friend, with no hurt feelings. That is still within the bounds of what decent people might do. The Torah tells you, Don't do even that.

More positively, the verse means for us to actively help the deaf. If the law tells us that the deaf have certain legal disabilities, then morality tells us we must do something about that. For example, if we have concluded that a deaf-mute cannot contract a marriage or divorce, because he cannot effect a legal contract and say to his beloved, "I undertake to fulfill this contract with you, to support you, to love and cherish you," etc.—if we have determined that according to biblical law, this contract cannot be entered into by a deaf-mute—does that also mean that he cannot live happily with a woman? Of course it does not. So the rabbis instituted a *special* category of rabbinically sanctioned marriage even for the deaf-mute with a special marriage contract! An ordinary marriage contract says that "the groom has pledged his troth to the bride and has undertaken to support her and to provide her with such and such. And she has undertaken to provide him with such and such, and they made this compact, contract, bond." They don't have that power, according to the Torah? Well, they do, according to the rabbis, if the rabbis will vouch for them! So the rabbis instituted a rabbinically sanctioned marriage with a rabbinically guaranteed *ketubah*.

In the seventeenth century, for example, Rabbi Abraham ben Mordecai of Egypt refers to this special *ketubah* and gives us the text. It says something to the following effect: "So and so, the groom, who is a deaf-mute and cannot communicate in words, has indicated his desire to be the husband of so and so, a deaf-mute woman, who also cannot communicate in words. Since they can communicate only with a wink or a nod or other such gestures, therefore we, the *bet din,* the court, who are, by virtue of the Torah's teaching of compassion, *avihem shel haḥareshim,* the Fathers of the Deaf, the protective parents of the deaf-mute; it is we who have undertaken to guarantee this contractual relationship. We vouch for the promises made between bride and groom so that they should not be denied the happiness of living together, even though they cannot personally undertake the legal aspects of mutual commitment." This concept, *avihem shel haḥareshim*, that the court is the Father of the Deaf, is beautiful, even if paternalistic literally. It shows this grand compassion, this determination to help the deaf in whatever way they could. It is the duty of the court to assist them, and it teaches all of us that it is not enough to quote the law. We have an obligation to do something about legal disabilities; to do something to alleviate the plight of the disfranchised.

Then there are some interesting legal decisions on other ritual matters. The question of participation in a *minyan* is an example. Many of the rabbis who dealt with this have said that one who can talk even a little bit, if he can hear even a little bit, then he is as good as anybody else. But if he is totally disabled, totally deaf, and cannot hear to say Amen, he still counts. Let him come to the *minyan*. Others have made minor distinctions in this particular matter.

There are questions regarding possible violation of the Sabbath with regard to the use of the hearing aid. First, there is the prohibition against carrying things in the public domain on the Sabbath. May one carry his horn or his hearing aid? It is, after all, something other than a garment that is worn on the body; it is like carrying an object, which, according to the law, is forbidden on the Sabbath. But in the matter of a hearing aid for the deaf, there was no dissenting voice among the authorities in recent centuries who have ruled upon it. A person who needs a cane to help him walk may use the cane on Sabbath; a person who needs glasses to help him see certainly may wear the glasses. Therefore, the hearing aid may certainly be worn. Some rabbis recommend that the amplifying control be sealed up before Shabbat, so that one does not touch the electric controls. But none say that a deaf person should be denied the use of a hearing aid on Shabbat because of the problem of carrying.

A more serious problem than carrying is the amplification even without touching the controls. In most Orthodox synagogues, a microphone is not used on Shabbat. This is a controversial question. This is not a matter of Orthodox vs. Conservative or Reform, it is a matter of Orthodox vs. Orthodox. Many Orthodox rabbis in the Baltimore area, for example, have concluded that there is no violation of the Sabbath in the use of a microphone which is set before the Sabbath. Even if changes in voice volume cause electrical amplification, there is no violation in the use of a previously set microphone. Now the hearing aid certainly amplifies, and it is much like a microphone. But one of the extreme Orthodox rabbis, Yaakov Yitzchak Weiss, author of *Minhat Yitzchak*, of the *Eidah Hareidit* of London (for whom the chief rabbi of London is not Orthodox enough), has ruled that whereas most Orthodox synagogues do not use a microphone, and probably should not, the hearing aid for the deaf is an entirely different question.

A hearing aid is for the person's basic well-being. First, it is a danger to life if you cannot hear properly. You cannot cross the street properly. It has been shown that accidents that happen to people who are hard of hearing are caused by the fact that although they looked before crossing the street, they were not able to hear a car coming from around the corner. The ability to hear well is thus important for our physical well-being, to say nothing of the nonphysical. Prevention of accidents, prevention of *sakkanah*, of danger to life and limb, is a very important consideration. You may violate the Sabbath, you may violate the dietary laws, in order to protect your life or health. Three cardinal sins—murder, worship of idols, adultery and incest—demand martyrdom rather than acquiescence. Otherwise, if your health is threatened on Yom Kippur, not only are you permitted to eat, you are commanded to eat. It is more important to preserve life than to observe the law of fasting on Yom

Kippur. It is likewise more important to preserve life and health by virtue of assistance to one's hearing even if it involves possible carrying or amplification of an electrical device on Shabbat.

Further proof of this point comes from another area. There are two classical responses in the nineteenth century about problems in sending a child to a school for the deaf-mute. Available schools were not under Jewish auspices, and they certainly did not have kosher food. The question was: Should you send your child to one of these schools, where he will be tempted to eat pork and all kinds of forbidden foods? Both of the rabbis who dealt with the question, including the Hatam Sofer, who had his qualms about it, had to conclude that if there was no alternative, if you could not supply him with enough kosher food from home, then one should temporarily suspend the concern for kashrut for this child. Later on, that can be corrected, but now it is more important for him to get the benefit of correction or transcendence of this defect.

In conclusion, I offer a polemical, tendentious point. I am tremendously impressed by the open-mindedness of the rabbis who see the realities of the deaf situation, who know their disabilities and how these have to be overcome by helpfulness and compassion on the part of the rest of us. I also see the need for action; that the deaf who remain with difficulties should not be denied access to ritual or to other events of personal, religious, or social life.

One good way in which we can accomplish what is essentially the thrust of this tendency in rabbinic literature is to do something dramatic. What Rabbi Rabinowitz said with regard to the *heresh* is very helpful: "Put him in the category of the 'potentially major.'[3] Right now he is minor, but potentially major. Put him in the category of the potentially able to do all kinds of things as long as he can communicate in one way or another."

I will go even further. In psychology and in physiology there is the law of compensation. A person who is blind develops his hearing better than the rest of us. A person who does not hear develops his sight and sensitivity better than the rest of us. I would go even so far as to say that those who are deaf have an advantage over the rest of us; because of that so-called disability they have "compensated" by making themselves far more alert and far more sensitive. I think we ought to take the view that the deaf are *more* able and *more* qualified than the rest of us to do so many things that we take for granted. We do things without paying proper attention because, since we have our faculties, we neglect to develop the alertness and the striving to compensate for a lack in one area or another. A dramatic way in which to deal with this is a linguistic one. I think the word *heresh* ought to be abolished from our modern vocabulary. We ought to create a new Hebrew word for the deaf, or for the hearing impaired. That will help us sever the nexus; break the connection between deaf people today and that terrible categorization of the *heresh* with either the *shoteh* or the *katan*. The best way to break that nexus, to sever that association, is, perhaps, to create a new word, something like *k'vad shmiah*, "one who is hearing-impaired." Both the severe and the minor impairments are still a hearing impairment. We ought to create a new Hebrew word so we will stop the use of a homonym. We should cease thinking of the *heresh* at its worst, of the category of total disability, and start thinking of the *heresh* of today with his modern techniques and fundamental changes. Revolutionary strides have been made in helping the hearing-impaired communicate. And if they can communicate then they are as good, if not much better, than the rest of us. Agudat Ha-hareshim should change its name, and we should change our attitudes, while we help bring about objective change in what we can do.

The Morning and the Evening Sacrifice
How to Be Represented in These Days: With Special Reference to Claims of Deaf Mutes in the Jewish Community

Reverend Doctor Nathan M. Adler

I am addressing you this day, my brethren, having a special purpose in view. You are aware that the deaf and dumb children of our poor have to be brought up in an asylum, where they have not the slightest opportunity of being trained in our faith, and of becoming acquainted with the holy precepts of our religion. On the contrary (without herein imputing any wrong intention to the managers of that institution), the children must naturally be taught in such a manner that, in after life, they become indifferent to, nay, even estranged from, our faith.

There is much and just indignation excited by the cruel injustice that is done towards our nation, when a child belonging to us is kidnapped from us and reared in a strange creed; is it not worse if we, with open eyes, suffer our afflicted children

Rabbi Adler was the chief rabbi of United Hebrew Congregations of the British Empire from 1845 to 1890. This sermon was delivered 28 January 1864, at Great Synagogue, Duke's Place, London. The following excerpt makes clear that the interest in the deaf Jew is not a new phenomenon of our presumably more liberal times. Rabbi Adler's plea for Jewish religious instruction could appropriately be made today in a number of sections of this country.

to be torn from allegiance to our Law? Is it not worse if we allow them to be instructed in another religion, and to be turned aside from the faith of their fathers with the first gleam of intelligence that beams upon them? Surely, all our feelings of piety and humanity must revolt against our calmly allowing these poor children to be lost to Judaism. We do not so much blame the poor parents who are so unfortunate as to have children thus grievously afflicted. They are glad to find an institution where, by the help of able tuition, the spark of heavenly reason may be elicited from the minds of their children, so that the distressing fetters which are placed upon them may be burst asunder. The parents will naturally, like a sinking man, catch at every straw to find help. But is it not, I ask you, the bounden duty of the community to be a boot to the lame, an eye to the blind, a mouth to the dumb, and an ear to the deaf? The Lord asks Moses, "Who hath made man's mouth? or who maketh dumb, or deaf, or seeing, or blind? Do not I, the Lord?" Must we not feel that Providence has inflicted that calamity upon some of our fellow creatures in order to rouse within us the holy feeling of sympathy, so that we may stretch forth a friendly hand to save and to heal? Has not the Lord commanded, "Thou shalt not curse the deaf, nor put a stumbling-block before the blind." Do we not act in violation of this commandment when we allow these poor children to grow up in utter ignorance of their religion? Is it not the duty of the whole community to be moved with compassion, as erst was the daughter of Pharaoh, and to say as she said, "This is one of the Hebrews' children." Is it not a duty incumbent upon us all to take these children, and to nurse them for the Lord, so as to educate them that, as the prophet tells us, "on that day the deaf may hear the words of the book"? Then we may also hope that He will give us our wages, and grant us His heavenly reward.

I deem it a subject worthy of the most earnest and anxious consideration of the community, that an institution be established, be it ever so small, for the training of our poor deaf mutes—either independent of or engrafted as a branch upon one of our existing charities. Say not, there are already so many charities and institutions in our midst, the burden of maintaining which rests upon a few; why add another? I answer in the words of our sages, "God desires each of us to do according to his ability." What our brethren in Holland and in Austria can do, we in England surely can also do. (There are excellent Jewish institutions for the deaf and dumb both at Rotterdam and Vienna.) By accomplishing this we shall especially act in conformity with those three great fundamental precepts of our religion of which I have spoken to you. We shall bring up those poor children in the belief in *one* God; we shall love our neighbors as ourselves, and we shall bring an offering of a sweet savour unto the Lord. There are, I am happy to say, many brothers and sisters in our community whose names are household words in the abodes of woe and wretchedness, and they will joyfully lend a helping hand. We are not going down to Egypt for assistance; we lean not on a broken reed, but on those who have clear heads to understand, warm hearts to feel, and energetic hands to carry out every object that can conduce to the welfare of their brethren. And I feel persuaded that such an institution as I have described will shed a cheering hopeful light upon the gloomy prospects of some forlorn family, it will make the widow's heart sing for joy, and will raise the bent head of a sorrowing father. Bring, therefore, my deaf brethren, your sacrifice in the morning and in the evening, and the Lord will vouchsafe to you His glorious blessings. "Even as the new heaven and the new earth which I will make shall remain before me, saith the Lord, so shall your posterity and your name remain."

Keynote Address to the Second Congress of the World Organization of the Jewish Deaf

Rabbi Shlomo Goren

It has been my privilege to attend the First World Congress of Jewish Deaf. I learnt a lot at that Congress, and the Congress influenced me in decisions on the legal status of the deaf in accordance with Halachah.

In the past, the legal status of the deaf has, indeed, been inferior, because communication with people devoid of the natural capability of hearing and speaking was undeveloped. As president of the rabbinical courts, I have recently had to deal with appeals by deaf people, and I have come to realize how close they are to hearing and speaking people: as far as intellect is concerned, they are equal to the hearing. What has been lacking for mutual understanding was a means of communication. Now that this has been developed through reading, writing, and sign language, I am convinced that from a halachic point of view we can give the deaf virtually equal status to the hearing and speaking, except in cases requiring

Rabbi Goren was Ashkenazi chief rabbi of Israel. The views he enunciated at the Second Congress of the World Organization of the Jewish Deaf, in Jerusalem, in August 1982, represent substantial religious authority, though not dogma, for practicing Jews.

27

actual speech, when we must take into account that the sounds made by the deaf must be turned into speech.

In any case, I can assure you that we consider you as members of the Jewish people with equal rights and obligations as far as Halachah is concerned. When questions such as being counted in a minyan or even personal status, marriage or divorce, arise, the development of communication between you and the rest of mankind enables us to deal with them. Schools, language, writing and reading—all these further the contact between man and man and will eventually overcome the legal, halachic differences that still exist between you and the rest of mankind.

Totally unconnected with this congress, I had to deal with a serious case today, a case of *halitzah*, in which the husband's brother, who had to perform the *halitzah*, is deaf and dumb. I am hoping to find a satisfactory solution in accordance with Halachah, because as a result of the development and expansion of schools for the deaf among both Jews and Gentiles in the past century, halachic literature has also progressed toward recognition of an equal status for the deaf.

In any case, Judaism considers you adults with full rights in every respect. I thus bless the congress organizers and your leaders, who work with great devotion in Israel, the United States, and throughout the Diaspora in the Free World to link the Jewish deaf to Zion and Jerusalem. You should know, here in the united city Jerusalem, that the State of Israel is the homeland of every Jew and of every one of you. Here you are being heard and understood, and there is willingness to give you whatever you require, naturally within the framework of our possibilities. Here you are at home, in your family, amongst your people.

May the Almighty bless your congress and all your deeds. May you continue to learn, develop, and struggle. On behalf of the Chief Rabbinate of Israel, I assure you that we shall come toward you and will no longer consider you as having an exceptional status. We will consider you as sons and daughters, men and women who are devoted to the people of Israel, the Land of Israel, the Jewish religion, and mankind as a whole.

What a Deaf Jewish Leader Expects of a Rabbi

Frederick C. Schreiber

To say what a deaf leader expects of a rabbi is an occasion made for platitudes. I could discuss for hours all the characteristics of a rabbi which are common demands of everyone, whether he is deaf or not. As a matter of fact, the main point here is not what the deaf leader expects of a rabbi, but rather what he thinks the deaf Jew needs and wants from his rabbi, and this is somewhat more complex. Speaking from my own experiences as a deaf Jew, there are a number of things which appear to stand out as strong problems where religious matters are concerned.

The first of these is the lack of an adequate religious education. There are only one or two schools for the deaf in this country that have any relation to the Jewish faith and even in these schools the opportunities available to the child to learn about his own religion are minimal. Being raised in the Jewish faith at home does not do much to solve the problem. The deaf child needs the same opportunity to learn the hows and whys

This paper was delivered to the second conference held by the National Congress of Jewish Deaf, in 1970, in New York. At the time he made these remarks, Dr. Schreiber was the executive director of the National Association of the Deaf. The text of his paper is reprinted from *A Rose for Tomorrow*, © 1981, with permission of the copyright holder, Jerome D. Schein.

of his faith as does any other child. He needs not only religious instruction, but also explanations as to why things are not always the way they should be. He needs to know why, for example, he does not always go home from school on Rosh Hashonna nor fast on Yom Kippur. He needs to know why his food is Kosher at home but not in school. But most of all he needs to feel that his faith has a deep and abiding interest in him and his welfare and that his rabbi is his teacher, his counselor, his source of comfort and advice in times of distress.

Deaf people live in a world that differs vastly from any other because the common medium that binds most people together is communication. Our world is an auditory one, and the inability to learn by auditory methods imposes a heavy burden on the individual which, so far, has proven barely tolerable. Helen Keller once noted that if she had to do it all over again she would devote her time to working with the deaf because "blindness cuts you off from things, while deafness cuts you off from people."

It is this isolation that needs to be broken down and it is in this area that the rabbi can be of most help. A good Christian friend of mine once told me that it is impossible for a deaf person to fully integrate into the world of the hearing. This man had good speech, good lip-reading ability and he said: "I tried this (integration) in my church. I felt that if I could succeed anywhere, that would be the place because in church, people are *consciously* kind."

Whether or not my friend is correct is immaterial for this paper. The point is that there are very few avenues through which any deaf person can get sympathetic understanding and help for his problems. The deaf Jew needs to have someone to turn to in times of stress, someone who can counsel him, comfort him, guide him not only in religious matters, but with secular problems as well.

Most communities have an abundance of social service agencies which cover the entire spectrum of human needs. But if the Washington Community Survey is any indication, none of these agencies are equipped to deal with deaf persons. Few have personnel who can even communicate with deaf people. Even fewer have people whose knowledge of the psychology of deafness, the educational background and childhood development of the congenitally deaf person is adequate enough for effective counseling.

When the deaf Jew needs help, can he go to his rabbi and get it? Right now the answer must be "no." But he ought to be able to do so. What's more, the concept of seeking help from this source should be instilled in early childhood, so that when one grows older, one will instinctively think of one's rabbi in times of stress.

This, of course, poses problems. Few rabbis are any more familiar with the deaf than are the social service agencies mentioned previously. It may be unrealistic to expect that every rabbinical student be required to familiarize himself with what is an admittedly complex subject when the chances that he will have deaf people in his congregation are minimal to say the least. Still, it is not unreasonable to suggest that such students be advised to seek help from more knowledgeable people before attempting to give guidance, should the need arise. The deaf person can quickly recognize that his advisor is not familiar with the complexities of his disability and turn away, rejecting not only the advice but the advisor and perhaps even the Temple itself.

It does not seem far-fetched to suggest that rabbis be alerted to this problem and advised that the National Congress of Jewish Deaf be contacted as soon as one discovers there are deaf Jews in one's congregation. Then the Congress could provide lists of referral agencies and other sources of information that are available to the rabbis. Such professional help as psychiatrists, interpreters, social workers, etc., is available and can be secured when needed.

Where there are deaf Jews in a congregation the rabbi might

assume a major role between the deaf person and community service agencies. In particular, the State's Vocational Rehabilitation Agency and the counselor assigned to the deaf person. While Rehabilitation Agency counselors may know a little more about deafness than the average rabbi, generally this is only a smidgen more and the counselor, over-burdened with a heavy caseload to begin with, cannot give his deaf client the time and attention he needs. But a rabbi could—he has, generally speaking, few handicapped people in his congregation and even fewer who need the kind of help the deaf individual requires. Thus, working with a Vocational Rehabilitation counselor, the rabbi could do much to help that counselor provide real service to his client. He might be able to ease communication difficulties, help with some of the formalities involved in processing a case, such as making medical appointments, hearing tests, or whatever is needed to help the client.

Religious leadership is another area where one would hope that the rabbis might exert a positive force. In my own community in Metropolitan Washington, there are enough Jews for at least special services on occasions such as Rosh Hashonna, Yom Kippur and Passover. This situation exists in other communities as well, but such services are seldom held. One might wonder why don't the deaf people themselves move in this direction? And that would be a valid question. The answer might be, first, that we have never received any encouragement to do so. Then there is the problem of communication; a deaf Jew can't just pick up a telephone and find a Temple or a rabbi who is willing and able to arrange for such services, nor can he easily reach the other members of his faith to convey the information. Finally, the quality of leadership varies from community to community so that truly effective leadership on the local level is scarce. Most deaf people are underemployed so that even the community leaders are severely restricted in what they can do; all are volunteers with very limited resources.

These are but a few of the things one expects from one's rabbi. Perhaps a great deal of attention should be focused on the children of the deaf. They are seldom considered, but they have a far-reaching effect on Judaism. All evidence has shown that the deaf Jew has been sadly neglected by his religion. How, then, can he be a functioning member of his own congregation and also insure that his hearing children will be brought up in the faith of his fathers?

When I tried to enroll my children in Sunday School in Montgomery County where I live, I was told I had to be a member of the congregation, and despite my pointing out that I would derive no benefit from such membership, I was told "it would make my children feel better" if I joined. So I joined. I asked only that my children's teachers be made aware that I was deaf and did not have the training necessary to fulfill the role of a typical Jewish father. This did no good because my children were continually coming home with questions that their teachers had told them to "ask their father." These questions, of course, I could not answer, which embarrassed both me and my children. So I refused to continue as a member of this congregation and took my problem to a Reformed Temple hoping for more understanding. Here I was told by the rabbi that he was more interested in me than in my children. But I knew at that time there was little he could do for me, although, if my children had proper training, proper contacts, it was possible, even probable, that when they grew older they could interpret for me at the Services and thus bring me back in the fold. Since this was not to be, I had a private tutor to complete their religious education because it was never a matter of cost but rather of principle that motivated my actions. My sons were Bar Mitzvah but they never really had the social or religious contacts which lead to regular attendance at any Temple. At this time, two of my children have married Gentiles. The other two will probably do the same. This hurts. Whether he attends a Temple or not, whether he is deaf or not, a Jewish boy who grows up in a Jewish household, is still a

Jew. And I began to wonder—how many families are there in the same situation as I? If the deaf Jew is not important to the Temple, certainly his children and his children's children should be and their future is worth considering.

Larger cities have deaf congregations. New York, Philadelphia, Chicago, Los Angeles, all boast of congregations of deaf people. All have regular services for deaf Jews and some may even make provision for the children of their members, but not enough is being done, not for the hearing children of deaf parents, not for the deaf children who live in all parts of the country, not just in the big cities and even in the cities where there are deaf congregations, all too often the impact is lost by the use of lay readers, interpreters and the like. The deaf Jew is reasonable enough to understand why an interpreter might be needed where only a few deaf people are involved. We do not really believe that every rabbi should or would learn to communicate with us in our own language, but we do think that where the congregation is large enough this should be done. We should be able to get rabbis who are thoroughly familiar with all aspects of deafness, who can communicate with us in our own language, and who can instill in us a feeling of trust and security.

For our deaf children, there should be a more intensified effort to see to it that they get proper religious training. It is disheartening to note that when reading over the literature on education, there is, if not frequent, at least regular mention of what is available for Christians—and almost nothing—I say almost to be conservative because I have found nothing at all—about programs for Jews. I don't care whose fault this is and I would not even want to speculate on whose responsibility it is to insure that something is done to provide our deaf Jewish children with adequate religious training. It seems to me that if religion is important, then it is the responsibility of those primarily concerned with religion to see to it that the children are not neglected.

It is fairly certain that there is at least one Temple located in those communities that contain residential schools for the deaf. Many of these schools may have only a few Jewish children but they are there. For the most part the children, perhaps, are en route between the school and their homes on Fridays; they generally live too far from the school to return to their homes for the holidays, Jewish holidays that is; so they get no attention at all. Why can't the Temple take the initiative in seeing to it that the children get adequate training? I am sure school administrations would cooperate, and that interpreters could be found to assist the rabbis in this important task if it were undertaken. When one stops to consider that it is not only the deaf child who is being lost to Israel, but also his children and his children's children, the effort necessary appears justified. After all, aren't we *all* the Lord's Chosen People?

The Deaf Person and the Jewish Community

Alexander Fleischman

Permit me to offer a poem as an introduction.

How We Look at Things

Being sad or happy often springs
From merely how we look at things.
It we feel mean, we only see
The very worst of what can be
But if we have a cheerful heart
And keep it that way from the start
Than all that might have brought despair
Will never come, for warmly there
Our will to see the better side
Will find us better satisfied.

—Hadley W. Smith

It is perfectly fitting that a deaf Jew be invited to write on behalf of the Jewish deaf of America. It is perfectly fitting that a

Mr. Fleischman is the executive director of the National Congress of the Jewish Deaf and president of the World Organization of the Jewish Deaf. He writes with the authority that comes from these exalted positions and from his personal experience as a deaf Jew.

deaf person undertake this role, mainly because he/she has the insight, the evaluation, and the sensitivity of the whole situation and the foresight to recommend improvements in it.

In 1972, the National Congress of the Jewish Deaf, with a grant from the U.S. Department of Health, Education and Welfare, conducted a workshop on "Orientation of Jewish Clergy and Leaders to Deafness and Vocational Rehabilitation." It was a truly educational course for those who had little or no knowledge of deafness. Interesting seminars about deafness and Judaism were held in 1977, at the First Congress of the World Organization of Jewish Deaf, and again in August 1982, in Jerusalem, at the Second Congress of the World Organization of Jewish Deaf. The significant moment in the latter came when Israel's chief rabbi, Shlomo Goren, declared in his keynote address that, in his observation of and research on deaf Jews, he was confident that they qualify for all rights and privileges as members of the Jewish community and called for the removal of all barriers.[1] The WOJD was inspired by this recognition from the chief rabbi of the Land of Our Fathers. However, one wonders how far his words have carried. How many American rabbis have heard of this declaration and accepted it?

In the International Year of the Disabled, the New York Society for the Deaf provided another welcome occasion to do some soul-searching about relations between deaf and nondeaf Jews which are not as they should be. It is hoped that from such discussions a better understanding of the Jewish deaf will emerge—as well as increased efforts to cope with their needs, their aims, and their involvement.

When we refer to relations with deaf Jewish adults, we must first take a hard look at the whole picture—past, present, and future—and review their status, their education, their religious practice, the Jewish community, rabbis, press coverage, and other categories. The final touch for a perfect picture is far from completion. It calls for a renewed effort to understand and to unite the deaf and the Jewish communities.

An important point is to determine the number of deaf Jews in the United States. According to the National Census of the Deaf Population, in 1974, there were almost 500,000 prevocationally deaf persons in this country. Let us claim at least 5 percent of this figure, which gives us close to 25,000 deaf Jews.

From whichever angle we look at this number, it indicates that the deaf are very much the sons and daughters of Abraham, Isaac, and Jacob. They are part of our heritage, followed by their offspring and the generations to come. And yet the deaf of America are the most overlooked and forgotten group of handicapped people by our Jewish community. We often envy the attention and support given to the blind, the lame, the mentally retarded. We often wonder why the deaf continue to remain at the bottom of the totem pole. Do our hearing peers continue to believe the deaf are clannish, living in a "silent world" as second-class citizens? Or perhaps there are not enough indications of how far the deaf have advanced in the last five decades. Does the communication gap still exist? If our hearing counterparts are so enthusiastic about attending continuing education programs, why do they not elect to learn sign language—just as a foreign language? And if there are worlds to conquer, the 25,000 Jewish deaf could constitute a greener pasture. Judaism challenges man not simply to accept his grandfather's opinion, but to continue to search and change. Religion and Jewish community hold before man the greatest values he has ever dreamed.

Deafness is an invisible handicap as compared with other disabilities. You cannot identify a deaf person walking down the street—until you speak to him and he points to his ears and shakes his head in the negative. Next you will see him taking out a pad and pencil, or perhaps he tries to speak in a high-pitched or hoarse voice. Your first impression is that the deaf person is weird, mute, uneducated, and communication between you and him comes to a halt. The deaf person is always underestimated in capability and intelligence and underrated in society in comparison with hearing peers.

We have come a long way to upgrade the educational and self-supporting status of the deaf. There are over 400 day and residential schools and at least 10 colleges for the deaf in America. You will find hundreds of college graduates plus a good number of Ph.D.'s among their number. Our deaf rank-and-file members hold important positions in schools, colleges, state and federal government offices. Many are in executive and supervisory positions in private industry. A surprisingly good number manage businesses of their own. There is no question that deaf people have treaded across rough roads to establish a comfortable identity in society. The abilities to speak and lipread, or the lack of them, should not be factors in attitudes toward deaf people.

By now, many readers may be thinking: Why are not Jewish deaf people more exposed to and involved with the Jewish community? What are they doing to promote their Jewish heritage?

One of our holy books, the Talmud, which was written 2,000 years ago, says that women, children, and deaf people cannot take an active part in performing many of the commandments. There are historical and religious reasons for this which might have been tolerated 2,000 years ago, but cannot be justified today. This ancient law was changed several years ago by Reform Judaism, but the concept is so deeply rooted in Judaism that many Jews are unaware of the change.

Those deaf adults who attended residential schools far from home had limited religious education, tutored by volunteers among the teaching staffs. Those schools located in small towns seldom have a rabbi, and the nearest temple is usually far away. Ofttimes there are no Jewish religious programs, and the Jewish child innocently participates with Christian children in their Bible classes. The picture is far different for the Christian deaf students. Every denomination is represented with ordained or lay people, fluent in sign language, to give spiritual guidance to the youngsters. Lacking the breadth and depth of instruction about Judaism, many deaf Jewish adults lose their Jewish identity. They intermarry, assimilate, convert. Ofttimes, some become easy prey to Jews for Jesus and other such movements. And when I look back to my religious education at the New York School for the Deaf, I must thank my teacher, Meyer Lief, who forty years ago taught me what I know about my religion.

A greater number of deaf adults, more sensitive to their heritage, are able to cast their lots in social, cultural, and religious programs among the seventeen Hebrew congregations of the deaf in principal cities of the United States. With limited techniques and without financial assistance from outside their ranks, these congregations struggle to make ends meet from meager dues and fees earned by social events. They may have High Holy Day services and a Passover Seder officiated by an ordained rabbi who is assisted by an interpreter. Or they may depend upon one of their leaders to officiate. The deaf Jews have inhabited a religious world barren of many of the aspects of religious practice that are so familiar to their hearing brethren—a private Jewish world, separated from the American Jewish community. It is indeed a tragedy.

Yes, a private Jewish world, with a great void existing. The deaf lack insight and training for wholesome Jewish community life. Participation in large philanthropies, like UJA and Bonds for Israel, or in fights against the oppression of Soviet Jewry is almost nil. The hearing temples and other Jewish organizations do not make an effort to recruit the deaf membership, as they do the other handicapped groups, nor have they tried to establish rapport with those who approach them. At the same time, many of the deaf have been zealous to retain their identity. Can you envision the deaf rubbing elbows with their fellow Jews in temples, sisterhoods, brotherhoods, B'nai B'rith, National Council of Jewish Women, Hadassah, and other such organizations? With proper guidance, the deaf could serve on committees and assist their hearing-impaired kinfolk on larger scale within the framework of these above-named national organizations. Their participation would educate the Jewish community about their capabilities for living, working, and sharing together. This is what Judaism should be, and is, about.

In Jewish life, a rabbi is the influential person spreading leadership and inspiration. With insufficient rabbis for the deaf, one wonders about the future plight of the Jewish deaf with the services of only half a dozen rabbis in the nation. How can rabbis have the proper coordination and communicate with the deaf when seminaries do not offer courses in deaf education, counseling for the deaf, history of the deaf, and training in the language of signs? Rabbi Douglas Goldhamer, of Bene Shalom Congregation, in Chicago, said, "Sign language gives life to my hands."

Lastly, why are seminary requirements so severe for deaf candidates for the rabbinate? One of the functions of the NCJD's Endowment Fund is to provide instructors to teach student rabbis the sign language. After ordination and job placement outside the deaf community, the good training and hard-earned money is often wasted. It is the same repeated ball game when a new rabbi is assigned to the group: he learns a bit, becomes competent, and leaves for a better-paying post.

On the other side of the coin, the deaf share in the pitfalls that prevent their joining the larger Jewish community. Their leadership in each vicinity has not spoken up loudly enough to gain attention. There has been a lack of involvement in Jewish causes to gain recognition for their enthusiasm. Knowing from experience the kind of religious education they received in their youth, deaf adults have not made efforts to better the situation for the young deaf students. They have not sufficiently publicized religious services to gain the attendance they should have.

Taking all of these problems into consideration, we again must fan the flames for improved relationships between the

Jewish community and the Jewish deaf. Results do not come from hoping and dreaming. The bridge has to be crossed by both participants, locked arm in arm. Let me close with an eight-point program to change deaf Jews from the overlooked and forgotten to *involved* deaf Jews.

1. An improved deaf awareness program within the Jewish community.
2. Better rapport between the Jewish community and deaf leaders.
3. More qualified teachers in religious education across the nation for youths as well as adults, including Torah studies and youth counseling.
4. Appointment of deaf paraprofessionals to work with rabbis.
5. Inclusion of deaf adult leaders as speakers at meetings of the Jewish community.
6. Establishment of sign language classes with deaf teachers.
7. Consideration for the needs of deaf Jews in Jewish community projects.
8. Persuade hearing children of deaf parents to become rabbis and/or community leaders and serve the deaf.

When Moses came to Pharaoh, he did not speak in negative tones, he did not simply say, I don't want my people oppressed. Moses put his proposition positively. He said, "Send forth my people that they may be actively involved in the community in which they serve."

Need a Jewish deaf leader say more?

Note
1. For the full text of Rabbi Goren's speech, see above, p. 27.

Maintaining Jewish Identity in the Modern Society

T. Alan Hurwitz, Ed.D.

When I received a request from Dr. Waldman's office a few weeks ago about addressing this topic to rabbis and other spiritual leaders for Jewish deaf people, I began to ask myself what it means to be a deaf Jew in this modern society. I did ask myself whether I am a Jew first and a deaf person second, or was it the other way around? I thought about what it means to be a deaf Jew in a large metropolitan city, in a small city, in a rural area, or even in a large city where the general population of Jewish deaf people is small or comprised mostly of mixed marriages. Finally, I pondered the question of how a deaf person can maintain his Jewish identity in this modern and complex society. How is it possible for any Jewish deaf person with very little or no religious background to maintain his strong Jewish identity as a result of the complexities of social, economic, and moral values in the society. In most places there is a lack of trained personnel and support services in the Jewish community to provide proper guidance and resources to the

Dr. Hurwitz was president of the National Association of the Deaf at the time he wrote this article. He is the dean of students at the National Technical Institute for the Deaf, which is housed at Rochester Institute of Technology, New York.

development of Jewish heritage for deaf people. In this paper I will share my personal experiences in maintaining my own Jewish identity, as well as that of my family's, in this complex society. I also will discuss some of the ways in which you and the deaf community can work together toward common goals of the Jewish community.

In spite of the limited opportunities for deaf people to receive formal education in Judaism, I continue to be amazed that many deaf Jewish people are able to maintain their Jewish identity in one way or another. They observe most Jewish holidays, e.g., Rosh Hashanah, Yom Kippur, Chanukah, and Passover. Many of them do observe Sabbath with candles on Friday evenings and attend temple services regularly. Some of them maintain a strict kosher diet and use particular dishes for Passover. This reminds me of a story about a deaf Catholic priest who was born a Jew and preaches in South Africa. Father Axelrod once desired to be a rabbi but couldn't get any encouragement or help in this goal. He still celebrates the Sabbath before lighted candles with his mother. He helps the Jewish deaf people in South Africa by serving on a committee in their organization.

I am also reminded of another story which may portray a typical Jewish deaf person. Once there were two wealthy and highly respected merchants from New York. Messrs. Levine and Moskowitz made their first visit to Israel. They dropped into a Tel Aviv night club where a comedian was having a great time entertaining the audience. His entire rendition was delivered in Hebrew. Mr. Levine listened to it in silence without cracking one smile, but Mr. Moskowitz roared with laughter at each skit. When the comedian was finished for the evening, Mr. Levine said to Mr. Moskowitz, "You certainly enjoyed that fellow's program. I did not know you understood Hebrew." "I didn't understand one word of it," answered Mr. Moskowitz. "If that is true," countered Levine, frowning, "how come you laughed so much at what he was saying?" "Aha!" beamed

Moskowitz, "I trusted him." This reminds me of the time when I attended Orthodox Jewish Services with my parents, who are also deaf. We just sat there in the synogogue and stared into space. We had prayer books with us and tried to look industrious. We were reading, but we did not know what was happening during the services. I remember asking my father how he could stand the silence and mystery during the services. He just told me not to worry about it and to be at ease with myself. I guess he was trying to tell me that he trusted the rabbi and other friends in the temple. We smiled at others frequently and made cordial nods to them. That was all. We had faith in Judaism even though we did not fully understand it.

This brings me to a funny incident that occurred a few years ago when many cars had bumper stickers of all kinds. Some of them said, "I found it!" Others said, "I lost it!" Still others said, "I never lost it!" Maybe we should be saying that deaf Jewish people "never lost it," but need help.

To this day my parents are still reverent in their Jewish faith although they lived in a small town in Iowa for over forty years where there were only sixty Jewish families and no other deaf Jewish people in the town. Recently, they moved to Kansas City, where there is only a handful of Jewish deaf people. My father continues to attend an Orthodox synogogue by himself almost daily.

Neither my father nor I were Bar Mitzvah, nor were we confirmed at our temples. My father's father immigrated from White Russia, where his father was a religious leader. When my grandfather discovered that my father was deaf, he excused him from Judaic studies. It has been traditionally said in the Torah that a man has to have perfect senses (ability to hear, see, etc.) in order to be able to pursue the rigors of Judaic studies. Otherwise he is excused or put aside as being "incompetent" and unable to learn. When my grandfather discovered that I was also deaf, he gave me the same excuse. In spite of this, he continued to include my father's family in all of his Jewish activities. We participated in their Sabbath dinners as well as Passover Seders. We did not understand a word that was being said. He spoke mostly in Hebrew and Yiddish. My parents and I just went along with them. We respected them a great deal and did not wish to create any upheavals. My grandmother loved to bake breads, pies, and goodies. She made them for us, her brothers, and their families every week. She was a lovable and simple lady. My grandfather loved all of us and never reprimanded us for driving or buying things on Sabbath and holidays. My grandfather loved to tell me many stories about the Old Testament, but I could not understand all that he said. I remember one time when a Catholic friend came to visit us at my grandparents' home. She had a picture of Jesus which fell out of her purse. I picked it up and showed it to my grandfather, thinking he would blow his stack. He simply said that Jesus was a good man and a good friend to the Jewish people.

Although my wife had better training as a Jewish child than I did, she participated in the religious education program against her own wishes. She started attending the religious school when she was six years old and was the only deaf student there. She did well, but she tells me that she cannot remember what she learned in the classes. Her classmates were required to attend a certain number of Friday night services and give a written summary of each sermon to the rabbi. Because there were no support services for her at the temple, Vicki was unable to comprehend what the rabbi was saying. Her father, bless him, went with her each time to write notes of the sermon for her. Vicki was active in the B'nai B'rith Girls (BBG) and held chapter and regional offices. I too was involved in the Aleph Zadik Aleph, but I was active only in the athletic programs. In the meetings of the AZA, I served as sergeant-at-arms because it was the only office in which I could contribute to the chapter communicationwise. Although my wife had more Jewish experiences than I had, she admits that she has not fully accepted her Jewish role in participating in the temple activities as much as I do. She resents being a hypocrite for attending temple services and not understanding very much even with interpreting services. I guess I just accept it because of my father, who showed so much tolerance under these circumstances. However, my wife and I try to observe our Jewish faith as much as possible at home. We feel that our home is a good place to practice our Judaism and that a temple is not the only place to worship, especially if we do not feel a part of the temple congregatioin.

My wife and I had a blissful wedding at a temple. We had a bris party for our son, Bernard. We did not have any interpreting services because we did not think of it during the earlier days, therefore we really did not know what was being said at these ceremonies. Bernard is now twelve years old and is hard of hearing. He attends a Jewish religious school, is learning Hebrew, and brings home projects. Before my grandfather passed away at the age of ninety five three years ago, he had hoped he would live to see our son becoming Bar Mitzvahed next year. He was so pleased that Vicki and I could help our son to gain his religious education. However, I must share with you that it is not an easy task because my wife and I cannot help him at all with his Hebrew nor with the history of Judaism. We often received notes from our son's Hebrew teacher that he needs to practice Hebrew more at home and that we should encourage him to do so. How can we do this when we do not know Hebrew? Our son hates to go to temple services because he has difficulty hearing prayers and sermons even with his hearing aid. The temple is not accoustically designed for hearing-impaired people, so our son argues with us every time we take him there. He refuses to use an interpreter; maybe it is due to peer pressure and not wanting to be different from his hearing peers. We discussed it with our rabbi and, bless him, he told us not to make our son hate being a Jew himself. The rabbi was willing to excuse our son from the required attendance at the temple services. He agreed to let Bernard continue to attend religious classes on Sundays and Hebrew classes on Mondays without specific attendance requirements. Recently our son was elected to serve as class representative on the student council at the temple. He is well on his way to becoming Bar Mitzvahed. He has a stronger understanding of the Jewish heritage than we do! Whether he will continue his religious training beyond this level is completely up to him, we promised him.

Vicki and I adopted a sixteen-month-old deaf girl, Stephanie, from the Jewish Family Services in Boston six years ago. We tried to give her an early start in Judaism education at the temple two years ago. The rabbi willingly hired someone to act as a special education teacher for her, but we soon realized that she was not yet ready. We are hoping that someday there will be a special religious program for Jewish deaf children in Rochester. The Bureau of Jewish Education in Rochester had considered setting up such a program, but nothing as yet has been accomplished. There are not enough Jewish deaf children in Rochester to justify such a program. We will continue to explore this possibility with our rabbi. He has demonstrated a willingness to provide interpreting services for deaf people in his temple. He performed a beautiful ceremony for the Hebrew naming of our daughter a few months ago. He arranged to have the temple take care of the expenses for an interpreter fee. We are optimistic about our rabbi's willingness to help and about the future educational opportunities in Judaism for our children.

In Rochester there are approximately twenty five Jewish deaf people of which only six to ten have attempted to organize a group to provide social and cultural opportunities for deaf people in the Jewish community. The group is known as the Hearing Impaired Chavrah (HIC) and meets monthly to plan activities around Jewish holidays. The Jewish Community Center of Rochester has been very generous in helping us with our logistical needs. We hold most of our meetings and parties at the JCC. Sometimes we meet in the homes of our members. Through our rabbi, the HIC members participated in the Yom Kippur services with an interpreter. Last year the HIC coordinated a religious retreat with the Hillel chapter of the National Technical Institute for the Deaf (NTID) at the Rochester Institute of Technology (RIT). Approximately fifty people participated in the two-day retreat. It was a rewarding experience for everyone. Rabbi Lynn Gottlieb of New York City led the services for us. The HIC is affiliated with the National Jewish Congress of the Deaf and has hopes of expanding into a strong group for Jewish deaf people in upstate New York.

There is a tremendous opportunity for the Jewish community and Jewish deaf people to work together and achieve a viable Jewish life for deaf people. It is not reasonable to expect that deaf people will fit into the Jewish community without special support services or modification in the temple services and programs. There are barriers which need to be removed. Interpreting services alone will not solve the problem. There are attitudinal problems which require a great deal of effort and education to help the general population to be more aware of the special needs of deaf people. Learning sign language is one way that hearing people and deaf people can begin to communicate with each other. Deaf people vary in their communication skills, English language abilities, and experiences in Jewish life. Deaf people do not need sympathy or pity. We despise paternalism. We need help, true, but not in the sense that people need to hold our hands or treat us like babies. We simply want challenges and opportunities.

There are several specific ways in which rabbis and the Jewish community can be resourceful in the development of Jewishness among our deaf people and children, thus helping us to maintain our Jewish identity in this complex society:

1. Support the concept of designing and providing special temple services for deaf congregatioins.

2. Provide interpreting services to deaf congregants, as required, at the expense of the temple.
3. Provide religious education to deaf Jewish youngsters.
4. Provide continuing education in Judaism to Jewish deaf adults.
5. Train rabbis and other spiritual leaders about aspects of deafness and the special needs of Jewish deaf people.
6. Provide sign language classes to hearing people in the congregation.
7. Install telecommunication devices for deaf people in temples and Jewish Community Services.
8. Consult the National Congress of Jewish Deaf and the National Association of the Deaf for their resource assistance.
9. Use Jewish Community Centers as a resource for deaf people in the Jewish community.
10. And many more as deemed appropriate for deaf people.

In summary, Jewish deaf people are as human as anyone else! We are capable of doing a great deal for ourselves and living independently. We have jobs, families, homes, drive cars, pay bills and taxes. We can do many things that you are normally capable of doing. We are frustrated because we cannot lead a complete Jewish life without your help and support. Communication is our main problem; there are other obstacles like language differences and limited experiential opportunities in Jewish life. We call on you to be aware of our frustrations and needs. We haven't lost *it*, but we are the lost characters in the Jewish Heritage.

I appreciate your giving me this fine opportunity to share my experiences and insights with you. As I look at you, I have a warm feeling that here is a tremendous opportunity for you, deaf and hearing people, to work together in the growth and preservation of the religious spirit of the Jewish deaf community. Here I salute my long-time friend, Alexander Fleishman. He has worked a good many years in upgrading the quality of life for Jewish deaf people and is still bullying his way through. Every time I see him I feel bad that I didn't jump on his bandwagon, but I hope to do so someday when I am wiser and more patient with the trials and tribulations of developing Jewish heritage for deaf people in America.

Religious Training for Deaf Youths

Meyer Lief

My experience with giving religious instruction to young people began in 1932 at what was then Fanwood and is now the New York School for the Deaf, in White Plains, New York. Although I had success with this work, I became more and more discouraged as my efforts continued. It is true that I prepared many boys for Bar Mitzvah; most of them had the ceremony at the Hebrew Association of the Deaf headquarters, some at their hearing parents' synagogues. The reason I became discouraged was that so many pupils left the classes without good reason and they were not interested. What bothered me was that their parents tacitly approved their abandoning religious instruction.

I resigned from teaching Bar Mitzvah classes in 1942 because of a change in my regular job. When I retired from work, in 1969, I again started teaching religious classes. But many changes had happened at Fanwood and I could not do very much. By now students had "released time" at 2:15 in the afternoon, and they preferred sports to religious classes, so

Mr. Lief has retired from a career in industry. An active member of the Hebrew Association of the Deaf for over half a century, he has led an exemplary religious life. He was appointed by the Hebrew Association of the Deaf as a religious instructor of deaf youths, enabling many of them to enjoy the rite of Bar Mitzvah. He has also worked assiduously to bring religious services to other Jewish adults who share his deafness.

they just disappeared. The parents did not care, and I could not get good cooperation from the supervisors, coaches, or even the principal.

I was assigned by the New York Society for the Deaf to give religious instruction at Junior High School for the Deaf 47, in Manhattan, but by that time there were very few Jewish children there. The Jewish children seemed to go to the other schools, many of them to Lexington. But Lexington School, in Queens, would not accept me as a religious teacher, because I use hand signs to communicate.

Religious education is a difficult problem today, because so many Jewish children now live in Westchester and Long Island, New York, and in northern New Jersey. They go to different schools with special classes for deaf and hard-of-hearing students. You see, there are not enough Jewish deaf children in any one school to make a religious class.

Today, I no longer teach, but I would like to tell all Jewish parents of deaf children to try to give their children a good Jewish education. They should do this not by compulsion but by encouraging their children.

What I have told you so far is history of Jewish education for deaf youths in New York City. At this time, as I said, I no longer teach classes, but I know something about what others are doing, and I would like to tell you about it.

We have a Jewish day school for Jewish deaf children, under Rabbi Ebstein, as dean, and Mrs. Laura Nadoolman, as principal. Under the auspices of the Union of Orthodox Congregations, Rabbi Lederfeind has organized educational and social programs for young deaf people. Beth Torah of the Deaf has an educational program at the Avenue N Jewish Center, in Brooklyn. Also in Brooklyn, the Hebrew Educational Society gives religious instruction to deaf children in cooperation with the Brooklyn Hebrew Association of the Deaf. Lincoln Square Synagogue, in Manhattan, makes arrangements for interpreters for a few of its adult programs. Temple Emanu-El, in

Manhattan, has interpreters at its community Seders. Temple Beth Or, in Queens, has a religious school.

These recent developments are very welcome. However, there is much more to be done. For example, in White Plains, there are many wealthy, large congregations, but I do not know of any synagogue serving that area that has taken an interest in giving religious education to the Jewish students at the New York School for the Deaf, in White Plains. There are the same number and kinds of congregations in Queens and on Long Island, and yet I do not know of anything being done for the religious education of Jewish students at the Lexington School for the Deaf, which provides their secular education.

These are some of the problems facing those who wish to bring love of Judaism to our deaf children.

Ceremonials, Rites, and Worship

Rabbi Elyse Goldstein

I think that the topic of ceremonies, rites, and rituals for deaf Jews can be broken into three separate questions. The first is: Are there any differences between the ceremonies and rites of the deaf and hearing Jewish communities, and if there are, what are they? The second question is: How can Jewish professionals, and here I specifically deal with the role of the rabbi, effectively serve the Jewish deaf? The third question is: Where deaf Jews are not served by a larger support network of a deaf synagogue or organization, what can we do to help alleviate their spiritual and religious isolation?

Perhaps an anecdote will best serve to explore and attempt to answer the first question. When I first came to Temple Beth Or of the Deaf, I was immediately faced with the unique halachic, or legal, and the emotional and psychological needs of the deaf congregants. On Rosh Hashanah of my first year there, I was asked: "Rabbi, who blows the shofar?" Clearly the Halachah states that in order to perform this mitzvah for others who may hear, the shofar blower himself must hear the sounds, for the blessing is: *"Lishmoah kol shofar*—to hear the sound of the

As a student rabbi, Elyse Goldstein served Temple Beth Or of the Deaf and assisted the Hebrew Association of the Deaf in adapting religious services for its members. Her years in that position have given her insights that she graciously shares here. She is now a rabbi at Holy Blossom Temple in Toronto, Ontario.

shofar." Yet how could we deny the honor of blowing the shofar to our congregation's president? This was my introduction into the challenge of meaningful ceremonies and worship for the Jewish deaf. In all honesty our solution did not please everyone. I could have taken the responsibility upon myself to blow it, as a rabbi, but try as I would, after weeks of hard practice, still no sound would come out. We ended up asking the hearing son of our temple's treasurer to blow the shofar, as he was a skilled trumpet player. I offer you this anecdote not as practical advice, but rather, to demonstrate the thought process which occurs in the Jewish deaf community in terms of rituals. This was the first of many experiences which proved to me our synagogue's unique concerns in the area of ceremonies. Are there differences? Allow me to offer you three examples of our unique situation.

The first and most significant is, of course, language. The role of Hebrew and the simultaneous use of both voice and sign. Here we have small, practical considerations when using sign: Who holds the Kiddush cup? Who holds the Torah while I pray? Since it is difficult enough to sign with two hands, let alone with one, I cannot turn to face the ark during my own prayers unless the congregation is reading silently during their prayers. We have the question of the role of Hebrew. If I use Hebrew I also simultaneously sign the English meaning, so my congregants can lipread the Hebrew while seeing the meaning in sign. The language of our prayer book is also a consideration. It often lacks clarity, and its images are difficult to follow in sign. We pray to a God who "hears" prayer; on Rosh Hashanah we say *"Shema kolanu—Hear our voices"*; we say *"Shema Yisrael—Hear, O Israel."* For deaf Jews, to hear the shofar is also to feel its vibrations, and we add that to the traditional *brocha* on the holidays. "God pays attention to our prayers." *Shema Yisrael* can most certainly also mean "Understand, O Israel; take heed, O Israel; we know, O Israel."

The second unique consideration is our use of Judaism's

already rich treasury of visual symbols. We have a heritage of touches, smells, and sights which hearing congregations do not necessarily utilize. For example, on Simchas Torah, our entire congregation helps roll the Torah from Deuteronomy back to Genesis, and in doing so can experience the tactile sense of Torah, as well as hearing it read. The same is true in home rituals: lighting the menorah, using the Seder plate, and serving Shabbat symbols are all highly visual and lend a sense of connection to the tradition for a Jewish deaf family.

Our third consideration is the struggle for full participation of deaf Jews in services. Because of the visual nature of interpreting, it is possible to watch a service the way one would watch a play, and so the worshippers become spectators. This is a unique problem in an interpreted service. In a hearing congregation we sing; deaf congregants watch. We pray out loud, they watch. Responsive readings, sign-singing, tactile and visual resources, and clear and interesting language are all examples of efforts to *include* deaf persons in worship settings.

This brings me to our second question; for to have meaningful ceremonies for the Jewish deaf we must have Jewish professionals, especially rabbis and educators, who can serve them effectively. A familiar lament, over and over again, is that young, interested rabbis who serve deaf groups leave in rapid succession, sometimes even before they have mastered sign language. This is not necessarily the fault of the student rabbi, who cannot afford to live on a part-time salary after ordination. The Jewish deaf community, on the other hand, cannot afford full-time professionals. Part of the solution is the outside support of the larger Jewish community, which should be seen not only as an obligation but a privilege. It would enable some Jewish deaf groups across the country to organize and support deaf synagogues, clubs, and Jewish centers. The other question relates to the special training needed by Jewish professionals, including an in-depth exploration of deaf culture and psychology, and the study of sign language. I would hope the interest generated by Hebrew Union College and its generous support of endeavors with the Jewish deaf across denominational lines will be copied in other rabbinic seminaries.

The third and last is the question, How can we serve the deaf Jew who may be isolated in a hearing community, whether large or small? How can we help to alleviate the feelings of aloneness and religious exclusion? In *all* cases, one theme is clear: whatever ritual problems, language differences, and lack of training may exist can be dealt with, if the attitude of the Jewish community changes.

Let me give you an example of the insensitive attitude: "Why teach the Bar Mitzvah boy or Bat Mitzvah girl Hebrew? They don't use their voices anyway. It's good enough for them to do it in English."

Last year, while trying to secure a *get* (Jewish divorce) certificate for two of my congregants, I saw this attitude over and over again in my search for a "kosher" document. What that attitude says is: Let the deaf be satisfied with substandard Judaism, less than satisfying life-cycle events, less than normative worship experiences. I submit that there is no longer room in the Jewish community for this attitude in terms of ritual and ceremonies of the Jewish deaf. Likewise, there is no longer room in the deaf community for it. I would like to offer you three concrete examples of how we can maximize the experiences of the Jewish deaf in ritual matters. I have chosen three life-cycle events to demonstrate these examples.

The first is in preparing for Bar or Bat Mitzvah. The deaf person can learn Hebrew via fingerspelling, sign, or orally, depending on the wishes of the individual. Reading Hebrew as they would read English, forming letters into fingerspelled words, such as *bah rooch;* providing that the person recognizes *bet-reysh-shoorook-chaf* as the word *baruch,* without having to orally say *baruch.*

Second, all life-cycle events should be arranged for optimum visibility, even if it means adding an extra platform. One must be especially careful at weddings. For example, I once stood on a small ladder so my hands could be seen under the *chupah*.

Third, one of the most sensitive moments of a person's life is at a funeral ceremony. There is something about the emotional and psychological power of the *Kaddish* in its original Aramaic language that the deaf person should not be denied. This is true for all events where Hebrew is used. The deaf person should be encouraged to stand next to the person reading the *Kaddish* or some other Hebrew prayer, and should say or sign Amen at the appropriate parts. Better yet, give the deaf person a copy of the prayer, either in transliteration or in Hebrew letters if the person knows how to read them, so they can follow along.

Perhaps with these small sensitivities, we can begin to do away with the terrible feelings of religious isolation some deaf families feel. The deaf Jew is no different from the hearing Jew in that he or she wants ceremonies and rituals, as well as worship, to have meaning and a sense of holiness, as well as a sense of correctness, measured by the standards we hold for all Jews. I hope these practical suggestions will be considered and both hearing and deaf communities will adopt the idea of shared responsibility to make meaningful ceremonies a reality through active participation, commitment, and a sense that we need never settle for what is less than attainable.

May God strengthen the work of our hands together.

Jewish Signs and Vocabulary

Rabbi Daniel Grossman

I would like to begin by saying that the title "Jewish Signs and Vocabulary" is very presumptuous. It implies that I, Dan Grossman, will create these signs. This is wrong on several accounts. First, it ignores the work already done by Alex Fleischman, Adele Shuart, Meyer Lief, and many others. Next it suggests that only a rabbi in the hearing community is capable or acceptable in creating new signs. This is inaccurate and insulting to the deaf Jew who has already formed a vocabulary of Jewish identity. Having clarified the seeds for possible misunderstanding, I wish to move forward and explain what I do see as a positive contribution to creating Jewish signs.

By Jewish signs, I refer to that vocabulary of holidays, rituals, life-cycle, and worship which even when participated in using only English language still retains elements of Hebrew which do not accurately translate to English. For example, in the other papers in this volume some words are left in Hebrew and may limit their communication's value. This includes

Rabbi Grossman holds a master of arts in religion and philosophy from Temple University and is a graduate of the Reconstructionist Rabbinical College, where he received his ordination. He served as assistant Hillel director at the National Technical Institute for the Deaf and as assistant rabbi of Temple Israel, Scranton, Pennsylvania. Presently he is rabbi of the Arden Heights Boulevard Congregation, Staten Island, New York.

61

concepts of Jewish belief and practice which shape our identity. For a deaf Jew, a lack of specific Jewish signs restricts one's ability to taste the rich flavor of Judaism. An example of that most definitely would be the words for "God" or "Jew." In English we generally use one word, *God*, or possibly *Lord*, and on occasion, the adjectives *Creator* or *Master of the Universe*. Here, it is the English which limits our vocabulary of prayer. When we use Hebrew, we open the possibility to forty different names and descriptions for God. Sign language, when it is merely a translation of English, shares the same limitations as English, and this limitation increases as we move further from the original language. The second example is the term *Jew*. It has the same limitations as we saw with *God*. In English, we limit ourselves to *Jew*, but in Hebrew literature we find the following: *Jew, Hebrew* (as in a biblical character), *the People Israel, Holy People,* and many other phrases which enhance and enrich our understanding of the basic term *Jew*. By increasing the variety of Jewish signs, we increase our access to ritual, prayer, and identity. As a side benefit, I believe that as deaf Jews develop and use more Jewish vocabulary, the non-Jewish deaf community will begin to form a clearer picture of the Jewish world.

If the issue were merely one of translation, then deaf Jews interested in the subject of Jewish sign need only to go to a Hebrew-English dictionary and look up the words, then sign the English side of the page. It is not that simple. In total, there are 100 to 120 "Jewish-Hebrew" words needed to fill out a Jewish identity. Simple translation leaves out the soul, the culture, and the deep roots of these concepts, and it is for this reason that they have not been translated from Hebrew into any language. Names of holidays, ritual objects, and value concepts have retained their Jewishness through their unique vocabulary and are left intact in English, French, Russian, or any other language. As example, Yom Kippur does not become "Day of Fasting," *yamulka* does not become "skullcap," and *bar mitzvah* does not become "youth of responsibility." When we go from Hebrew to English to sign we lose sight of the word because each translation is an interpretation as well as a language change. Rather than sign a parallel English word for a Hebrew concept, I suggest a totally new sign where possible.

Hebrew, as a language is based on the verb. Signs are based more on verb action than noun objects. English is primarily based on the noun. Therefore, if we were to go from Hebrew to a conceptual explanation to a sign, we would be more accurate than when we go from Hebrew to English to sign. As an example, let us take the word *shalom*. The dictionary reads, "Peace, tranquility, quiet, safety, welfare, comfort, greeting, salutation, etc." How, then, from that mixture of vague similarities, do you sign *shalom*? If, however, we do not list words but an explanation, we find that *shalom* is more than peace; it is welfare of every kind—personal, familial, national, and spiritual; it is the holistic balance of a person and his world. That explanation includes all the words, which after a time may not sufficiently suit the needs of language. If we move in the direction of phrases rather than specific words, we eliminate the problem inherent in English: inaccurate or dry words for rich, full concepts. We also allow for signs closer in content to the Hebrew. By using a variety of signs for "Jew" or "God," as the same example, we increase our understanding. Every rabbi and teacher complains of the repetition of the words *Jew* and *God* in prayer when a variety of word phrases would be much better.

Here is where I see my role in the area of Jewish signs and vocabulary. First, to help catalogue those 100 or more words used in Judaism which must have a usable counterpart in sign. Second, to develop concept definitions, so that deaf Jews, native signers, can then build on those phrases and develop their own Jewish vocabulary free from the problems inherent in English. Third, as a rabbi, to employ these signs, developed by deaf Jews, in the context of Jewish ritual so that these signs become part of Jewish life. It is my position that if these Jewish concepts and vocabulary move from Hebrew to sign concepts and bypass the standard English translation, which is usually out of date and lacking in emotional and spiritual content, deaf Jews can have avenues of worship and ritual equal to the beauty and depth of sign language.

Finally, I see the introduction of many of these signs to teach hearing Jews a visual component to difficult concepts. Rather than misinform our students that *shalom* equals "hello," "good-bye," and "peace"—which is nonsense—we may visually show a holistic concept of tranquility and increase everyone's ability to communicate.

A few years ago, I made a presentation to the Committee on Special Needs and Projects of United Synagogue. The result was a promise for support for preparation of educational materials for the Jewish Deaf Community to establish the means of production and distribution of this material, as well as a firm commitment that even as I or others work with the deaf community through the early stages, the Jewish deaf community will ultimately decide on the realities of any sign.

Jewish sign is one step toward Jewish identity. Together we can make it a truly meaningful vocabulary and not a mere reflection of Hebrew through archaic English.

Identifying and Meeting the Needs of Elderly Deaf Jewish Persons

Lester J. Waldman, J.D., LL.D.

During the seventeenth century, on the American continent, it is alleged that only 20 percent of the population reached the age of seventy. Today it is estimated that in the United States 80 percent of those alive will reach the age of seventy. While figures will vary from nation to nation, it is universally accepted that the life span everywhere is on an upward grade. With more people there are more problems, and with the enlarged aged population there are both more and new problems.

There is a well-worn definition of the Jew: "Jews are like everyone else, only more so." We can extend the description to the deaf community. "Deaf people are like everyone else, only more so." In other words, being Jewish and being deaf present an intensified aspect of the living process. That intensification is reflected most noticeably among the elderly.

Elderly deaf people are perhaps the most isolated of elderly people. They are isolated from the mainstream of the community as well as isolated from access to services within the community. Although in the United States there have been

A lawyer who has had a long association with deaf people, Dr. Waldman has served as a president and executive director of the New York Society for the Deaf.

many programs designed to meet the needs of the nation's elderly citizens, these services do not accommodate deaf people. This is largely because the providers of these services to the elderly have not developed the capability to communicate with deaf people. Therefore, many elderly deaf people are not even aware of existing services which are in the community.

Once again, communication becomes the focal point in the discussion of the problems of elderly deaf Jewish persons. The metropolitan New York area is the largest Jewish community in the world and, it is assumed, contains the largest number of deaf Jewish persons. Two institutions in New York serve deaf Jews. One of these is the Hebrew Association of the Deaf, with over 800 members, which is about to celebrate its seventy-fifth anniversary.

The other is the New York Society for the Deaf (NYSD), organized in 1911. Two things about NYSD should be noted. It was incorporated by a special act of the New York State Legislature in 1913, which gives it an unusual status. The second is that it probably is the only agency under Jewish auspices in the United States that offers generic services to the deaf community. Financed primarily by the Federation of Jewish Philanthropies, its general services are open to all deaf persons regardless of religious preference. There are two reasons for this policy: the Jewish and American traditions of not turning anyone away, if the person has a need that can be filled, and the fact that some of the society's programs are underwritten by government funds. Although it cannot undertake every responsibility, the breadth of NYSD's program is indicated by service in the following areas: sponsoring Tanya Towers, an apartment building for elderly deaf people; programs of personal and family counseling; job placement; scholarships for deaf graduate students at New York University; advocacy and legal assistance; summer camping for deaf children and elderly adults; sign language classes; a central bureau for interpreting services; psychological testing; and substance-abuse prevention and remediation. Special attention is given to deaf people who have additional disabilities, particularly those who are deaf-blind.

In addition, NYSD has a specific Jewish program. This includes providing office and meeting space for the Hebrew Association of the Deaf and its sisterhood; arranging for Rosh Hashanah and Yom Kippur worship services and the Passover Seder; a monthly Shabbat service followed by an Oneg Shabbat lunch and religious discussion period; maintaining the Shalom Youth Group for teenage Jewish boys and girls; counseling services for Jewish parents of deaf children; and a special weekly class to teach English and American Sign Language to Russian and Ukrainian Jewish emigres.

NYSD's board of directors includes persons who are deaf. The president of HAD and its sisterhood are ex officio members of the board. A sign language interpreter is present at all board meetings.

It may be gathered from the sweep of these activities that major needs of Jewish elderly persons living in the area are being met. However, there are many gaps which should be filled. This is the problem which we now address.

Mental Health Facilities

In the area of mental health there exist in New York City only two licensed services where both manual and oral communication are employed to diagnose severe emotional illness. However, there is little provision for family treatment, marital counseling, or any of the newer modalities being utilized within the hearing population.

The families of the hearing impaired, who are often at a loss to cope with their feelings regarding the handicapped person, must utilize existing mental health agencies in the hearing community. While this has been effective for families with other types of handicaps, the special nature of the communication problem between parent and child, hearing siblings and deaf siblings, and also hearing children and deaf parents, often is not understood by the counselor or therapist unfamiliar with the ramifications of early hearing impairment. In thinking about sensory deficits, most people think of deafness as simply an inability to hear.

Thus, the hearing-impaired individual may suffer from problems of isolation, depression, inadequacy, low self-esteem, and developmental lag. These problems can impair the psychosocial functioning of the family as a meaningful unit. With these conditions in mind, the lack of supportive services, such as counseling for families, is glaring.

Another of the deficiencies for elderly Jews is specialized counseling for the bereaved. Loss of the husband or wife member of a deaf couple is especially devastating. Not only is there grief but the loss of companionship means, in most cases, a loss of someone with whom to communicate.

Nursing Homes

Lack of specialized nursing home facilities is an especially troublesome problem. As age span increases, more and more deaf Jewish persons will be forced to seek places in nursing homes. This has already become apparent among those maintaining apartments in Tanya Towers. When elderly deaf persons are placed in nursing homes, they usually live in isolation with no one to communicate with. They cannot interact with other residents or staff and cannot participate in activities.

There is need to establish nuclei of elderly Jewish deaf persons in certain nursing homes to provide for social interaction and needs accommodation. Nursing home providers must be educated to the special needs of this population, particularly in terms of communication.

Homemaker Services

The current trend is to avoid, whenever possible, nursing home placement if independent living can be accomplished with homemakers to assist the elderly person. This means that there is a need for homemakers who know sign language and that some deaf persons should be trained as surrogate homemakers.

Housing

Despite all the publicity, NYSD's housing project, Tanya Towers, has received, it must be remembered that it consists of only 130 apartments. There is a long waiting list for the apartments, and no other housing has all the necessary features to specially accommodate deaf persons. The need for additional housing is a pressing problem.

Recreation Needs

Although many elderly deaf people attend deaf clubs, there are limited activities in these groups. For elderly deaf people, traveling to locations where they meet is very difficult. Many deaf people would be interested in going to existing senior centers, but fear and reluctance hold them back. When a deaf person attends a senior center, he or she is usually the only one in such a program who uses sign language and thus cannot effectively participate in the programs due to communication and attitudinal barriers. For deaf people to be integrated into programs, there is a need for at least one staff member to learn sign language or to use an interpreter. This would help in one-to-one communication and in programs and classes. Some programs should be designated for visual entertainment.

Medical Needs

There is a need to ensure access to medical services for elderly deaf people to the same extent as is provided to their hearing peers. In the United States, this is mandated by both law and regulations. Elderly deaf people should learn their rights for interpreting services and how to use an interpreter in a medical situation. Orientation about deafness should be provided for hospital staff. Beth Israel in New York now has a full-time sign language interpreter on staff. Other hospitals should be urged to do the same. Mount Sinai hospital now has a telephone service adapted for use by deaf persons (TTY). About fifteen other hospitals, including Beth Israel, use NYSD's TTY service in a cooperative arrangement.

The Deaf-Blind

In the entire Jewish community, deaf-blind people have probably been among the most neglected. NYSD is engaged in a pioneering effort to create a program of services for elderly deaf-blind persons. Their problems are special. Their mode of communication is special. Their service needs are special. No Jewish social service program can be deemed complete unless elderly deaf-blind people have been sought out and their needs responded to.

Conclusion

In investigating future needs of elderly Jewish deaf people, and in the planning for the fulfillment of those needs, particular attention must be paid to the necessity of having deaf persons themselves involved in the total process. They are the bearers of two prongs of disability: they represent a deaf minority group, and they represent a Jewish minority group. Without their total involvement, programs devised *for* them rather than *by* them will be arid and sterile.

One lives in a fool's paradise if one believes that the mere cataloging of social and physical needs is the equivalent of fulfilling those needs. The cataloging is only the introduction of a process. Not to be overlooked in connection with all of these considerations is the effect of another social change. In the United States, and undoubtedly in other nations as well, the family structure has changed. Gone is the three-generation family of children, parents, grandparents. In that matrix there was interaction: the gaining of wisdom and experience *by* the young *from* their elders, and the receiving of new ideas and emerging concepts *by* the elderly *from* the young members of the family group. In many instances, the young and middle-aged family members have fled to the suburbs and left their elders in the old neighborhoods of the core city. From this factor has come the growing practice of shunting aging family members to homes for the aged, retirement colonies, and nursing homes. No longer do we subscribe to the imperative: "When we were young they watched over us; now that they are old, we must watch over them."

In confrontation with the future it must be reemphasized that the subject of our concern is a group which stands in two minority positions. Solutions which apply to problems of the general deaf community may not always be applicable to the Jewish deaf community. Conversely, solutions to specific problems of the Jewish community may not always be applicable to the Jewish deaf community. Thus, those entrusted with the social planning have a particular responsibility to observe. That responsibility must be accepted and responded to in the highest tradition of the Jewish faith.

An Audiological View of Deafness

Maurice H. Miller, Ph.D.

The terms *deaf* and *deafness* require clarification. While the New York Society for the Deaf is devoted to the most severely affected sufferers of this condition, my concern as an audiologist extends to all persons with varying degrees of what I prefer to call *hearing impairment*. Hearing impairment is more widespread than deafness and represents the single most prevalent chronic physical disability in the country today. About 16 million persons have a hearing impairment of sufficient severity to interfere with social, vocational, and professional pursuits. So we see that when we consider the population who have sustained a significant degree of hearing impairment, we address a sizable segment of the population.

We use the term *deaf* to describe persons who do not have sufficient residual hearing to enable them to communicate entirely by auditory means, even with the most powerful hearing aids available. While hearing aids are extensively used by deaf persons, at least during the formative educational years, the auditory channel does not constitute the primary means of communication for them. The New York Society for the Deaf is unique in its charge to serve persons without

Dr. Miller, a distinguished author and lecturer, holds a doctorate in audiology and the position of professor at New York University. In addition, he is the chief audiological consultant at Lenox Hill Hospital in New York City.

functional residual hearing. These deaf people account for about 2 million persons in the United States. The term *hard of hearing* is used for those who, despite a significant hearing impairment, communicate primarily through the auditory route, with or without hearing aids.

Within the deaf population, we make distinctions based on the age at onset of the deafness. *Congenitally* deaf persons are those born deaf; *prelingually* deaf persons are those who lost much or most of their hearing in the first year or two of life. *Adventitiously* or *postlingually* deaf people are those who were born with normal hearing but lost most or all of their hearing after speech and language developed normally. The age at which a person becomes deaf is an important factor in assessing how the inability to hear will affect his or her life.

The Impact of Deafness

Let us consider the impact of deafness. Loss of hearing interferes with the ability to understand speech. That is a serious handicap, because our society depends for communication primarily on speech—an auditory event. When deafness is suffered prelingually, development of speech is often delayed or absent. To audiologists who have encountered some success in achieving intelligible speech with children who have little or no functional hearing, we must take exception to any recommendation that all deaf children need instruction by educational procedures designed for those who cannot hear. In children having residual hearing through the speech-frequency range (500 to 2000 Hz) in at least one ear, it has been my practice to recommend an oral program of education which emphasizes maximum use of amplification and residual hearing. When no residual hearing is measurable above 500 Hz, I believe the child should be placed in a program in which sign language will be used in addition to input from the auditory and visual channels.

As an audiologist, I have concentrated on identification,

diagnosis, and initial management steps. But hearing impairment affects virtually every aspect of life, from the need to be awakened in the morning by a vibrating alarm system to control of disabling tinnitus at bedtime. Between arising and retiring each day, hearing impairment impacts relentlessly on life experiences: radio, telephone, television, dictating machines, hearing the nocturnal cry of an infant, conducting a conference, conversation at the dinner table, applying for a job, and on and on to almost every activity in our oral-aural communication-oriented society.

Management of Hearing Impairment

The management of hearing-impaired persons requires more than the services of any single discipline. Many specialists are involved in identification, prevention, measurement, diagnosis, and rehabilitation. Unfortunately, too often specialists tend to see hearing problems only from their own point of view, and the coordination and integration of services that deaf people should have are inadequate. Audiologists are concerned with early detection and diagnosis and with the selection of suitable hearing aids. In pursuit of these objectives, we often overlook the important contributions that must be made by other specialists to achieve the level of rehabilitation that deaf people deserve.

We recognize various stages which parents of deaf children and persons who become deaf experience. The sequence of reaction is (1) shock, (2) denial, (3) sadness and anger, (4) adaptation, and (5) reorganization. These stages are normal and are often accompanied by feelings of bewilderment, fear, anxiety, sorrow, self-pity, and helplessness. Counseling is needed to ease these persons through these stages and to prevent their fixation at stages preceding eventual adjustment to the loss. Organizations like the New York Society for the Deaf, which provide counseling among other services, fulfill an important role in the management of deafness.

In negotiating our complex city, deaf people also encounter numerous frustrations because of their communication handicap. If they have a need for social services, their hearing handicap poses a formidable barrier to obtaining them. That is why the communication services of the New York Society for the Deaf are so vital to them. In similar ways the professionals who meet deaf persons must be aware of the very broad effects of deafness on the afflicted individuals' lives.

Conclusion

It has been said that the health of a society can be gauged by its care and concern for its handicapped citizens. By this criterion, we are a seriously ill society. For example, only 21,000 deaf children out of 46,000 are receiving the special educational services they require. Fifty-five percent are not. The situation is even worse when we examine the figures for hard-of-hearing children. Eighty percent are not receiving such necessary services as auditory training and speechreading. Similar figures for hearing-impaired adults are no better. Our society funds services for blind people far more generously than it does those for deaf people and, for the partially hearing group, almost not at all. So we can see that hearing-impaired people and their families must contend with more than their sensory deficit and its profound implications for the development of speech and language and interpersonal communication. They must contend with a society which is essentially unresponsive to their needs.

Some Demographic Aspects of Religion and Deafness

Jerome D. Schein, Ph.D.

How do prelingually deaf individuals fare in various churches? What are the attitudes of Catholics, Jews, and Protestants toward those of their members who cannot hear and often do not speak? Are special provisions made for their education? their participation in services? their leadership in the church?

Religious Preferences of Deaf Adults

Few studies have been conducted to determine the proportions of deaf persons who prefer a particular religious faith. Conversely, there are no published studies of the numbers of any church's membership who are prelingually deaf. One of the few studies of the former type queried the deaf population of metropolitan Washington, D.C., as to their religious preferences.[1] The Washington survey was an attempt at a total ascertainment of the adult deaf population; i.e., an effort was made to locate and interview *all* deaf persons who were eighteen to sixty-five years of age, noninstitutionalized, residents of metropolitan Washington, D.C., and unable to hear and understand speech through the ear alone. The survey located

Since 1977, Dr. Schein has been president of the New York Society for the Deaf. He is professor of deafness rehabilitation at New York University.

and interviewed a total of 1,132 persons of an estimated 1,492 deaf adults.

Each of the 1,132 persons was asked, "What is your religious preference?" Their replies are shown in the accompanying table. In addition to that question, follow-up questions were asked to determine their church affiliation and the amount of their participation in religious affairs.

Ninety-two percent of those interviewed expressed their preference for one of the Judeo-Christian religions. Only 10 persons in the sample (less than 1 percent) elected a non-Western religion (Hinduism, Mohammedanism, etc.), and 7.1 percent of the respondents gave *no* religious preference, either so stating (6.2 percent), identifying themselves as atheists or agnostics (0.1 percent), or not responding at all (0.8 percent).[2]

Not surprisingly, the largest single denomination was Baptist, accounting for more than a fourth of the total (27.5 percent). Roman Catholics made up the second-largest contingent (18.9 percent), followed by the Methodists (13.3 percent) and Espiscopalians (11.0 percent). Altogether, the Protestant groups made up a little over two-thirds of the total (68.4 percent). The number of respondents identifying themselves as Jewish was 4.5 percent. At the time (ca. 1965), a study of the area indicated that the Jewish population of metropolitan Washington, D.C., was about 5 percent of the total.

Differences by sex and race, also shown in the table, are generally unremarkable. The white males opted for Roman Catholicism first and the Baptist church second; the white females reversed those two choices. But for both nonwhite males and nonwhite females the first choice was the Baptist church, being the preference of nearly two out of three, as would be expected from a knowledge of the local population. Thus, it would appear that deaf persons' religious preferences are distributed similarly to those of the general population of the area.

Religious Preferences[a] of Respondents: Metropolitan Washington, D.C.

Denomination	White		Nonwhite		Total	Percent[b]
	Male	Female	Male	Female		
		Number of Persons				
No preference	39	23	5	3	70	6.2
Atheist, Agnostic	1	—	—	—	1	0.1
Baptist	80	111	61	60	312	27.5
Brethren (Church of the Brethren)	1	2	—	—	3	0.3
Christian Church (Disciples of Christ)	—	1	—	—	1	0.1
Christian Deaf Fellowship	1	2	—	—	3	0.3
Church of Christ	5	3	—	—	8	0.7
Christian Scientist	3	2	—	—	5	0.4
Congregational Church	—	1	—	—	1	0.1
Eastern Orthodox (Russian)	—	1	—	—	1	0.1
Episcopalian	62	63	—	—	125	11.0
Greek Orthodox	—	2	—	—	2	0.2
Interdenominational	2	4	—	—	6	0.5
Jehovah's Witness	—	—	—	1	1	0.1
Jewish (all)	26	25	—	—	51	4.5
Lutheran	33	34	—	—	67	5.9
Methodist	68	68	6	9	151	13.3
Mormon	1	3	—	—	4	0.4
Pentacostal	2	—	—	1	3	0.3
Presbyterian	13	15	1	—	29	2.6
Protestant (unspecified)	21	16	3	4	44	3.9
Roman Catholic	89	97	12	16	214	18.9
Seventh Day Adventist	1	1	—	—	2	0.2
Unitarian	4	4	—	—	8	0.7
Universalists	—	1	—	—	1	0.1
Other religion	2	3	2	3	10	0.9
Not reported	4	5	—	—	9	0.8
Total number	458	487	90	97	1132	100.1

[a]The figures in this table represent the responses to the question "What is your religious preference?" As this question was most often asked by signs and fingerspelling, its precise wording varied. In all cases, every attempt was made to ensure that the respondent understood the intent of the question.

[b]Of all respondents.

Church Membership

Expressing a preference for a religion is not the same as belonging to a church representing that religion. In the deaf sample, almost one-third of the respondents (30.7 percent) indicated that they were not members of any church group, though they considered themselves to belong to, or have a preference for, a particular religion.[3]

Deaf females more often than the males stated that they had joined a church. About three-fourths of the white females (75.2 percent) and a little over six out of ten white males (62.6 percent) compared to a few less than three-fourths of the nonwhite females (73.1 percent) and somewhat over two-thirds of nonwhite males (68.1 percent) named a church they had joined. It would appear that deafness per se is not a barrier to church affiliation.

Religious Practices

To what extent did those claiming church membership participate in the affairs of their churches? Nearly three-fourths of those who said they were church members also stated that they did *not* engage in any other activity than attending services—if that. When asked the follow-up question about the kind of participation, the one-fourth who indicated that they participated in some church activities were about equally divided between those who responded by mentioning some relatively minor activity (like baking a cake for a bazaar) and those who mentioned something fairly important (like holding a church office). Lacking comparable data for the general population, conclusions as to the probable effects of deafness on religious participation are not warranted. However, it would appear that for at least a small segment of the Washington deaf community—about 9 percent—deafness does not keep them from taking a major role in their church. This statement must be considered in light of the fact that there are several all-deaf congregations that are either affiliated with churches or stand alone, such as the Christian Deaf Fellowship. Obviously, in such congregations deaf people hold the dominant positions.

Religious Intermarriage

Deaf people typically marry deaf people. Most studies find that when deaf people marry they select a normally hearing spouse only once in ten pairings.[4] The rates are sex-and age-related. In the Washington study, of those males born deaf or deafened before six years of age, 91.9 percent have deaf wives; of those males deafened between six and nineteen years, 67 percent are married to deaf women. For women, 83.5 percent of those born deaf or deafened before age six have deaf husbands, and 56.9 percent of those deafened between six and nineteen years of age have deaf husbands. The comparable national figures for deaf people are similar, though rates for deaf-by-deaf marriages are somewhat higher nationally.

This tendency to select a deaf mate means greatly restricted freedom of choice. Since deafness tends to be a relatively rare occurrence in the general population, there are simply fewer deaf people from whom to choose. When the population is reduced by half (men marry women, and vice versa), reduced again by age (most marriages are between persons within ten years of their ages), and again by socioeconomic background (propinquity plays a large role here),[5] it is all the more remarkable that nearly two out of three marriages (64 percent) in the Washington study are between deaf persons who express the *same* religious preference. When the analysis is made by four broad groups—Catholic, Jewish, Protestant, and no preference—agreement in religious choices between spouses increases to 81.6 percent. The study did not inquire as to whether the high degree of agreement in religious choice reflected the couples' premarital statuses or a postmarital accommodation. Either, or a combination of both, might account for the findings.

By sex, the marriages between coreligionists were as follows:

68 percent Catholic men and 73 percent Catholic women, 67 percent Jewish men and 90 percent Jewish women, 91 percent Protestant men and 85 percent Protestant women. The numerically largest group, the Protestants, had the largest proportion of marriages between persons having similar religious preferences. But the data are not wholly consistent. Jewish deaf wives had the highest proportion of Jewish husbands. On the other hand, Jewish deaf husbands had the lowest proportion of Jewish wives.[6]

Moving from preference to participation, we find that the majority (88 percent) of deaf marital partners attended the same church regardless of their religious preferences. In 12 percent of the households, the husband and wife attended different religious services. These rates eliminate households in which only the wife attended services (13 percent), only the husband attended (7 percent), or neither husband nor wife attended (18 percent). The figures would suggest that in deaf households, as may be true more generally, substantial adjustments are made for religious differences between marital partners.

A matter of sizable import was not touched upon in the Washington study: when the parents have different religious preferences, in what religion are children raised? It should be recalled that the majority of the offspring from deaf-by-deaf marriages have normal hearing. Studies of children ever born to deaf couples have found about 10 percent of the offspring were deaf.[7] How do deaf parents manage the religious needs of their 90 percent normally hearing children? We have no demographic data with which to respond to this last question. It certainly deserves study. For some anecdotal evidence, the reader is referred to the essay by Dr. Schreiber (see above, p. 30).

Religious Instruction

The essays by Hurwitz, Lief, and Grossman in this volume

touch upon Jewish religious instruction. What about other religions? How do they address the problems of providing creedal perspectives to deaf children?

History records that Roman Catholic churchmen made major contributions to the education of deaf children. The first recorded instance of opposition to Aristotle's dictum respecting the teaching of deaf children was Pedro de Ponce, a Spanish monk, who successfully instructed several children of the nobility. Juan Pablo Bonet, another Spanish cleric, wrote the first book devoted to methods of teaching deaf students. In the eighteenth century, a giant emerged—Abbé Charles de l'Épée. This French priest established the first school open to all deaf students, not limited to children of the nobility. His methods spread throughout the world, becoming the basis for the education of deaf children in the United States.[8] Today, the Catholic church maintains nine parochial schools for deaf students: St. Mary (Buffalo), Holy Trinity (Chicago), St. Rita (Cincinnati), St. John (Milwaukee), St. Frances de Sales and St. Joseph (New York City), Archbishop Ryan (Philadelphia), DePaul Institute (Pittsburgh), St. Joseph (St. Louis).

The Lutheran church sponsors two schools for deaf children, one in Detroit and the other on Long Island. The absence of schools supported by Protestant groups probably should not be interpreted as a lack of interest in the religious lives of deaf children. Instead, most denominations do support efforts to provide religious instruction to students enrolled in public schools. These services are managed on a released-time or after-school basis.

The only Jewish religious school for deaf children in the United States is the Hebrew Institute for the Deaf, in New York City. Founded only a decade ago, the school is now in the process of expanding its enrollment to include students with a variety of other educationally handicapping conditions in addition to deafness. Of course, the schools for deaf students in Israel are both public and religious schools by the very nature of the government which supports them.

At the postsecondary level, the major faiths support religious activities at Gallaudet College, the only liberal arts college for deaf students in the world. Catholic and Protestant chaplains are assigned fulltime by their religious orders to the college. Jewish students are served by a parttime person from the community on a voluntary basis. The National Technical Institute for the Deaf, at the University of Rochester, makes no formal provisions for any religious group; however, the school's administration will assist Jewish deaf students in making local contacts with synagogues, if they desire them. Arrangements for the religious lives of deaf students in other postsecondary facilities that have substantial numbers of them have not been studied, but it is likely that the institutions do no more to accommodate the religious needs of deaf students than they do for those of students in general.

Deaf Ministers

In the United States, the Episcopal church leads all denominations in the preparation of deaf persons to serve as ministers. At present there are forty-five deaf Episcopal priests—all of whom lost their hearing before ordination—serving in various capacities throughout the country. Most have deaf-only congregations. In 1977, Rev. Thomas Coughlin became the first deaf Catholic priest. Other religious groups have one or more deaf ministers, with a few exceptions, such as the Mormon church. There are no deaf rabbis, though a young deaf man, Alton Silver, was studying for the rabbinate at Hebrew Union College (Cincinnati) when he died suddenly during minor surgery. While he would have been the first deaf rabbi, he would not have been, by far, the first rabbi to have an interest in serving deaf people. However, schools preparing rabbis, unlike some seminaries for other religious faiths, do not include information about deafness in the curriculum. Nonetheless, several rabbis are presently serving deaf congregations, either on a full- or part-time basis.

To what extent are clergymen aware of their deaf parishioners? One study conducted in a small town (Frederick, Md.) and a large city (Baltimore) found that many clerics were unaware of any deaf persons in their purview.[9] It is fair to speculate that few ministers, regardless of their faith, spend much time planning for or, better yet, actually serving deaf persons. The small numbers of any particular faith who are deaf, their relative "invisibility," and the difficulties in communicating with most of them are substantial reasons for the lack of attention given by the churches to deaf people. On the other hand, as noted above, most faiths have at least a few clerics whose special assignment is to serve deaf persons in their parishes. Whether the services made available to them are or are not adequate is a matter for the collective consciences of the individual religions.

Other Services

Religious groups have also been leaders in obtaining social services other than education. Ministers of various faiths have been leaders in obtaining family and child support, providing counseling services, developing recreation programs, and establishing homes for elderly deaf persons. The extent to which these activities for deaf persons have been under religious sponsorship varies greatly from denomination to denomination and from place to place. The Baptist ministry supports the Bill Rice Ranch, a national recreation program aimed at deaf youth. The Lutheran church in Minnesota has established a home for elderly deaf people. Many branches of Catholic Charities have special rehabilitation programs for deaf persons. Various denominations sponsor volunteer efforts that bring special services to deaf persons. These programs provide welcome additions to the array of social services for the less-fortunate members of the deaf community.

But what about the future? As the public becomes more aware of deafness, as government officials accept greater responsibility for meeting the needs of deaf and other handicapped persons, as the ability to improve the lives of deaf persons through various strategies and devices increases, what will happen to the role of religion in the deaf community? Monsignor Hourihan, in a learned disquisition on religion and deafness, sounds a warning note about, and proposes a revised view of, the religious role in the deaf community:

> As the church today faces greater fiscal problems as a result of declining membership, there will not be funds available to continue programs that are now servicing the deaf under religious auspices—schools, homes for the aged, rehabilitation centers, social agencies, hospitals, etc. The leadership of the church would do well to shift its policy from programming in some of these areas to an advocacy role whereby it will work and fight if need be to see that necessary programs are established by others and, if already established, to ensure that the deaf have their rights protected. Such an advocacy role should be developed in partnership with the leadership of the deaf so that it does not become a paternalistic role.[10]

Summary

No religion is without deaf members. The scant evidence available suggests that the religious preferences of the deaf population are very close to those for the general population. The proportions of Catholics, Jews, and Protestants in the deaf community are probably much the same as for the population at large. Similar findings might be expected for church membership and religious participation, though these matters have had little systematic study.

Despite the difficulties in finding a deaf mate of suitable age, education, and socioeconomic background, deaf people tend to marry persons with similar religious preferences in a bit over four of five marriages studied. Jewish deaf males have the largest rate of intermarriage among the couples studied, while Jewish deaf females had the lowest rate of intermarriage—a fascinating pair of statistics.

Having noted the similarities, discrepancies in the treatment accorded deaf persons by various religions must be pointed out. For example, Episcopalians in the United States have ordained far more deaf ministers than have any other religious group. Catholics, as they do for all of their children, make the largest contributions to education. Other denominations vary widely in their responses to the social and psychological needs of deaf persons.

More extensive and up-to-date information about the religious aspects of deaf persons' lives would be welcome. Little is known in a systematic fashion about how they manage the problems of interfaith marriage, of religious education for their hearing children, of understanding church services. More should be known about deaf persons' attitudes toward the religious groups with which they wish to affiliate and toward the treatment they are accorded by the congregations they may wish to attend.

Despite the small amount of data available, it seems reasonable to conclude that religion can play as vital a role in the lives of deaf people as in the lives of people in general. Whether or not deaf persons presently have the opportunity to enjoy full religious benefits is a matter at which demography can only hint. For those religions that recognize the problems imposed upon the instruction of and subsequent participation by persons deafened early in life, the value of further investigations should be manifest. Sufficient information about the religious lives of deaf people are simply not available. In turn, it should be noted that the responses of the various Judeo-Christian religions to early deafness are as diverse as are their other beliefs.

Notes

1. J. D. Schein. *The Deaf Community* (Washington, D.C.: Gallaudet College Press, 1968).

2. When interpreting these findings, the reader should bear in mind that the metropolitan Washington, D.C., area includes Gallaudet College, the only liberal arts college for deaf students in the world. Because of its presence in the area, the

proportion of deaf persons who are highly educated probably exceeds that for the nation as a whole. The federal government tends to be a favorable employer of physically handicapped persons, though branches of the civil service have proved to be less than hospitable to deaf workers. See F. Bowe, J. D. Schein, and M. T. Delk, "Barriers to the Full Employment of Deaf Persons in Federal Government," *Journal of Rehabilitation of the Deaf* 6, (1973): 1–15; J. D. Schein, M. T. Delk, and S. Hooker, "Overcoming Barriers to the Full Employment of Deaf Persons in Federal Government," *Journal of Rehabilitation of the Deaf* 13, no. 3 (1980): 15–25. Attracted to the area by the unusual educational and social opportunities it offers, students often attempt to remain in the area after graduation. These factors contribute to the unrepresentativeness of the deaf people in the D.C. area. Nonetheless, their lives are worth careful analysis, in order better to understand the meaning of deafness generally, and to appreciate its impact on religious life particularly.

3. The 69.3 percent who did say they belonged to a church did not include those who then failed to name the church to which they belonged; despite their affirmative response, they were tallied amongst those who were not members.

4. H. Best, *Deafness and the Deaf in the United States* (New York: Macmillan, 1943); Schein, *The Deaf Community;* J. D. Schein and M. T. Delk. *The Deaf Population of the United States* (Silver Spring, Md.: National Association of the Deaf, 1974). In their classic study of deafness in Northern Ireland, Stevenson and Cheeseman noted, "Presumably selection of similarly affected mates is due to social contacts at school and in later life and because deaf persons find greater relaxation in each other's company than they do with hearing persons." A. C. Stevenson and E. A. Cheeseman, "Hereditary Deaf Mutism, with Particular Reference to Northern Ireland," *Annals of Human Genetics* 20 (1956): 201.

5. The interviews revealed that in 36 percent of the marriages the couples had attended the same school at the same time—substantial support for propinquity and all that it implies about the factors influencing choice of spouse.

6. The small number of people involved (25 females and 26 males) does not encourage too much speculation, but the matter merits further study. Are Jewish families more protective of (or capable of defending) their daughters than their sons? Or can the discrepancy be explained largely by the fact that Halachah only excludes Jewish deaf males from ritual participation, while women are generally precluded by their sex, not by the state of their hearing? See Rabbi Feldman's discussion, above, p. 13.

7. Schein and Delk, *The Deaf Population of the United States,* found 88 percent normally hearing progeny of deaf-by-deaf marriages. The Washington study obtained a rate of 89.4 percent, and the New York State survey reported 90.4 percent normally hearing children of deaf marriages. J. D. Rainer, K. Z. Altshuler, F. J. Kallmann, and W. E. Deming, *Family and Mental Health Problems in a Deaf Population* (New York: New York Psychiatric Institute, 1963).

8. For more extensive accounts of the history of the education of deaf people, see R. Bender, *The Conquest of Deafness* (Danville, Il: Interstate Printers & Publishers, 1981); H. Lane, *The Wild Boy of Aveyron* (Cambridge, Mass.: Harvard University Press, 1976); and J. D. Schein, *Speaking the Language of Sign* (New York: Doubleday, 1984).

9. P. H. Furfey, a Catholic priest and a doctorate in sociology, conducted the study.

10. J. P. Hourihan, "Church Programs for the Hearing Impaired," in *Hearing and Hearing Impairment,* L. J. Bradford and W. G. Hardy ed. (New York: Grune & Stratton, 1979).

Appendix A

Selected Comments regarding Deafness from the Talmud and the Responsa

One of the remarkable features of Jewish religious laws is that their viability has been maintained over the centuries through decisions that have been made in specific cases by a great variety of rabbis in a broad range of circumstances. As questions have been posed about the application of the laws concerning a specific subject, their profound meaning emerges. Changes in circumstances have been reflected in different judgments: what may originally appear as an absolute dictum is shown, through the actual decisions rendered, to be less rigid than a literal reading might at first convey.

In an effort to further exemplify this aspect of talmudic law as it pertains to deaf Jews, some of the questions that have been posed to scholars at various times are presented below. Each group of questions and commentaries has been chosen to explicate an aspect of a complex issue. In making this selection, our intention has been to supplement the preceding learned papers, especially that of Rabbi Feldman, by giving this additional evidence of the great care the sages took when interpreting ancient wisdom in terms of current conditions. The citations also illustrate the depth of thought and the reverent humanism underlying the attitudes of the Jewish community toward its deaf coreligionists.

The citations that follow are drawn from a compilation of references to deafness in the talmud and responsa that was made by Rabbi Z. Ilani and B. S. Meir.

The original English translations are by Bryna Elman.

These in turn have been rearranged and somewhat modified by the editors. In doing so, we recognize the difficulties inherent in translations from one language to another, difficulties that are compounded by changes in linguistic conventions that have occurred over time. For scholars, the references for the citations will be found in the pages of the original compilation which are printed at the end of each of the quoted segments.

Is a deaf person who has been trained in a school for the deaf no longer included the category of "deaf" as our sages have defined that status? (A) What is the law applying to a person who is born deaf and mute but has been trained to speak? Does he remain as a person lacking intelligence? (B) Can a girl who is a deaf mute, has been schooled, but as yet does not speak though she occasionally makes strange sounds which can, at times, be interpreted as words be considered intelligent?
    A. There is a dispute among the important early authorities (Rishonim) concerning a person who was born with hearing but lost it afterwards. If the person in question is capable of speech, does he belong to the category deaf and dumb? Most authorities maintain that such a person does not fall into the category of the completely deaf and, therefore, his betrothal to a woman is valid. This decision holds only on the condition that he has been tested and can prove himself knowledgeable in his actions.
    B. Similarly, is someone born a deaf-mute who was trained to speak no longer in the deaf-mute category? The answer can be understood as dependent upon a dispute among the halachic authorities; therefore, there is a doubt whether the betrothal of a deaf-mute who was taught to speak is binding according to Jewish law. But in the case of the deaf-mute who did not actually learn to speak and only utters strange sounds, we

must certainly rule that she has not left the deaf-mute category and her betrothal is not binding according to the torah.

[Source: *Minhat Yitzhak* I:132: Rabbi Y. Y. Weiss (England, Israel, 20th century)]

Are the present-day deaf adults who study in special schools, learn to read, write, and understand people who speak to them (by lipreading and sign language), who can be employed as unimpaired people are, who speak in a somewhat grotesque manner which is difficult to understand, though they can be understood by someone who knows them well— are they to be considered deaf (in the category of the *shoteh* and minors) or are they judged as ordinary people? And if the latter, can they be made to perform *halizah;* that is, do the laws of levirate marriage apply to them?

There are those who say that the reason our sages consider deaf-mutes as not competent to fulfill everyday obligations is that, not being able to hear or speak, they cannot be taught. It is not possible for them to understand people's intentions clearly. Accordingly, a deaf person who is educated must be considered as an ordinary person. However, there are other authorities who have stated that our sages did not make distinctions between laws pertaining to deaf persons, but they equated all deaf-mutes and classified them as not competent to assume everyday responsibilities.

If the deaf-mute can speak, though grotesquely, is educated, and can understand a person speaking to him, as well as read, he must be judged as completely competent, according to all authorities. He may also be counted to achieve a quorum of ten men (a minyan).

Conclusion Our sages disagree as to whether a trained deaf-mute is to be considered intelligent, and no final decision can be made without pondering the particulars of an individual case. If the deaf-mute can speak, though in a grotesque manner, and if he has a clear mind, it is possible that all our sages will agree that he is to be considered competent. Therefore, he may perform *halizah;* i.e., the laws of levirate are applicable to him.

[Source: Decisions of the Israel Rabbinate, VII: 83 (file 189/27)]

Further on these points are some other twentieth-century discussions:

Five great rabbis of the generation of Rabbi Chaim of Tsanz (nineteenth century) ruled that a deaf-mute, having been graduated from a special school for the deaf, shall be treated in all respects as a hearing person. He is considered as a deaf person who has recovered, since he is competent to deal with everyday responsibilities. Other authorities of that period hold that there is a doubt as to the category into which such people are to be classified, deaf or hearing. Only a minority, among them Rabbi Chaim of Tzanz, maintain that such an individual shall be treated as completely deaf and that nothing that was done for, or taught to, that person will have an effect on whether the individual is competent. However, even Rabbi Chaim of Tsanz agrees that, if the deaf person developed a small amount of specch, he should be considered as having normal intelligence.

Rabbi Yitzhak Isaac Herzog's conclusion tends to the opinion of those authorities who rule that a deaf-mute who has been graduated from a special school and learned to read, write, and so forth, shall be considered as one of normal intelligence and in the category of a deaf person who has recovered. We need not bring proof from early authorities who assumed that there was no way to correct hearing impairment, even if we see that the deaf-mute is intelligent and understanding, because in those times techniques for teaching deaf people were not available; however, even in the Talmud we find mention of a deaf person who was healed.

Nowadays, the special schools for the deaf are to be considered as the means of cure. Especially in regard to those deaf persons who assume responsible positions among the general population. We should also note that Rabbi Toledano, chief rabbi of Tel-Aviv-Yafo, disagrees with Rabbi Herzog, who was the chief rabbi of Israel. The latter maintains that a deaf-mute who completed a special school is considered as still being the deaf-mute category to which our sages referred.

[Source: *Heichal Yitzhak*, I, E. H. II:47, Rabbi Y. Herzog (Ireland, Israel, 20th century)]

The obligation of a deaf person to perform good deeds *(mitzvoth)* and the obligation of a deaf-mute who was trained in a special school to perform mitzvoth.

Rabbi Simcha Bonim Sofer (Hungary, nineteenth century) answered: If the deaf-mute was educated in a special school for such people and learned how to speak with difficulty and with the aid of hand signs, he will be able to pray and deal with people and is, thus, obligated to keep all the mitzvoth as are the rest of the Jewish people.

However, another authority ruled in regard to a deaf-mute who was an expert tailor, who transacted business as a competent person, who knew the order of the prayers, and who was able to point out the prayers to others for the weekday, sabbath, and holidays was, nevertheless, considered a *shoteh*, since the rabbis have not made distinctions within classes; they have laid down the rule that the deaf person is not intelligent enough to assume everyday responsibilities; they have not distinguished between different deaf people.

Another authority, visiting a school for deaf-mutes in Vienna, closely observed the teaching methods at the request of the institution's management, and he was astonished by what he saw of the course of study and the students' behavior, to the point that he wondered whether it were not possible that these people were completely intelligent and therefore obligated to obey all the commandments. He requested that the school's management obtain phylacteries for all of the boys, in order that could they put them on every day.

[Source: *Shevet Sofer*, E.H. 21]

Can a deaf person blow the shofar? Is it not true that the commandment is to hear and not to blow the shofar? Therefore, if the deaf person is capable of blowing, why is he not able to fulfill the commandment by blowing? Why is he not considered obligated to do the commandment and thus is unable to help others in their performance?

The essential commandment of shofar is to hear or listen to the shofar, not blowing it alone. Proof of this is the Mishna which rules, "He who blows into a pit so that the sound is not heard is not considered as having fulfilled his obligations;" therefore, the benediction which is recited by the one who blows the shofar is "to hear the sound of the shofar" and not "to blow the shofar." It is for that reason that a deaf person who cannot hear is not obligated as far as the commandment of shofar is concerned.

[Source: *Har Zvi*, O.H. II:85]

Is a person deaf from birth who uses a hearing aid and is capable of hearing well with it, even things that are said in another room, and who has learned to speak by this means, though his articulation is not clear, be considered competent?

The Rambam, in his Commentary to the Mishna, Terumoth 1:2, attributed the inability of the deaf to speak clearly as due to their lack of hearing. Even if there is no reason or actual illness which keeps him from speaking, according to the Rambam (who was noted as a great doctor) the power of hearing is located in the brain and, therefore, the deaf-mute's lack of speech cannot be due to extensive brain damage. If he can speak and so has a means of communication with people, he can become competent in everyday matters and overcome his brain impairment with learning. But if he also is incapable of speech and has not had the opportunity to be with people, he remains in the category of the brain-damaged and is not considered competent.

According to this explanation of the Rambam, if the deaf-mute can speak by means of an electronic device, he can overcome the "brain impairment" caused by loss of hearing and can communicate with others. He should, therefore, be considered legally competent. However, he should not be considered a hearing person in all respects, since he hears by utilizing an electronic device and cannot hear in a natural manner. This case is not similar to the one involving a person who is hard of hearing and can hear when he is shouted at in a loud voice; it is not even similar to the case of one who hears with the help of an auditory tube, which was commonly used about 200 years ago. These types of people are not considered deaf but as hearing, because they actually do use their sense of hearing, even if it is not very good. This is not true of the deaf person who is aided by an electronic device. Such a person does not have any use of his natural hearing abilities; he acquires a new ability by using an electronic device as a medium but does not have a natural hearing ability at all, since he does not hear loud voices with the help of a special auditory tube which would bring sound to him.

From this we learn that a deaf person who hears with the aid of an electronic hearing device has the same brain impairment as a deaf person, but since he has learned to speak, his ability to communicate with other persons through speech overcomes his difficulties. He is, therefore, to be considered legally competent. He is considered a person who speaks but cannot hear and not a deaf-mute whose category is that of a *shoteh* who lacks the intelligence to deal with everyday responsibilities. According to the Rambam, however, one who can speak but not hear may not sell land, because for that one needs great cleverness and, since he does not hear, he is not clever enough for such activities. Therefore, the deaf person under consideration, who hears with the aid of an electronic device, may not sell land.

[Source: *Igrot Moshe*, E.H. II:33, Rabbi M. Feinstein (U.S., 20th century)]

Utilizing a hearing aid on the Sabbath and carrying it from a public domain to a private domain.

[It is prohibited to transfer objects from a private domain to a public one or vice versa on the Sabbath, except for the clothing one wears.] Regarding deaf people who wear modern hearing aids every day of the week and who would find it difficult not to use it on the Sabbath, we might say that it is somewhat dangerous for such a person to walk in the street without the device, because they rely on hearing more than on sight in order to avoid traffic accidents.

A lame person is permitted, on the Sabbath, to carry a walking stick that he requires as an essential aid to walking, and a nearsighted person is permitted to wear glasses. Similarly the deaf person is permitted to wear a hearing aid on the Sabbath, but only on the condition that it is impossible for him to go about without the hearing aid, just as the lame person cannot get around without the walking stick.

The writer also cites Rabbi Henkin's decision in his *Edut L'Yisrael* that the deaf who use an electronic hearing aid must prepare the device before the Sabbath and must anchor it securely so that it cannot be turned on and off; the part that one puts in a pocket should be sewn onto one's clothing.

[Source: *Minhat Yitzhak* I:37]

Concerning a person who hears with difficulty without a hearing aid, is it preferable that he utilize such a device to hear the reading of the torah, the megillah, and the blowing of the shofar, rather than attempt to do so without the aid?

There are those who hold that the act of listening with a hearing device is not the same as hearing the exact original sound, that it is more like hearing a reverberation (that is, an echo), which is generally held to be invalid. Therefore, it is preferable that the hearing-impaired person should draw closer to the source of the sounds and hear without the device as much as he can and should not utilize the device to perform these commandments.

[Source: *Minhat Yitzhak* I:37]

Appendix B

Facsimile of the *Prayer Book for the Deaf*, 1919

The reproduction which follows demonstrates that compassion for deaf Jews and an appreciation of their condition are not new. In 1919, the Council of Jewish Women published this prayer book in recognition of the difficulties imposed by deafness on learning English. This remarkable work is presented in toto for the benefit of those who may wish to make use of it in their religious services.

סדר תפלות ישראל

Prayer=Book

for

Jewish Deaf

COMPILED AND ADAPTED

BY

COMMITTEE ON WELFARE OF DEAF
COUNCIL JEWISH WOMEN

PHILADELPHIA
COUNCIL JEWISH WOMEN—Sole Agents
1919

FOREWORD

THE Committee on Welfare of Deaf of the Council of Jewish Women presents this book to meet a peculiar need. With the kind permission of the Central Conference of American Rabbis, a portion of the Union Prayer Book has been adapted to meet the requirements of our deaf for their weekly meetings, and also for home use in times of sorrow and rejoicing. Such prayers, psalms and responsive-readings were selected as in their judgment would cover the needs of the deaf. Simplicity of wording and clearness of meaning have been the chief aim in preparing this booklet. Our thanks are hereby extended to the Conference.

ROSE GOLDSMITH STERN,
Philadelphia, Pa.,
National Chairman.

Prayer=Service for the Jewish Deaf

Minister:

WE praise Thee, O God of the world, at whose word evening falls, and by whose will the gates of morning are opened. Thou hast made the changes of times and seasons, and ordered the ways of the stars in the heaven. Creator of day and night, Thou art God. Thou, ever-living God, will rule over us forever. Praise be unto Thee, O God, for the day and its work and for the night and its rest.

Thou hast raised man high above all other creatures and crowned him with honor, for Thou gavest him the power to choose between good and bad. Teach us, O God, so to live that we may become wise. Help us to do Thy holy will and to keep our minds free from wrong. Make us good and help us to do acts of love and kindness towards others.

As week quickly follows week, and man does not notice it, so pass the years away and the end of our lives draws near. May we so live that our souls will be pure and content and that at last we shall rest in Thy loving care. Amen.

1

(Congregation standing.)

Minister:

Praise ye God, to whom all praise is due!

Congregation:

Praised be God now and always.

(Congregation sitting.)

Minister:

WE praise Thee, O Lord, our God, Ruler of the world, who in Thy goodness causes light to shine over the earth and all its people, and daily creates new works. How many are Thy works, O God, how wise hast Thou been to make them all; the earth is full of Thy doings. The heavens show Thy wonders and the stars show Thy greatness. Thou makest light and darkness, bringest good out of bad, and bringest peace to the heart of man.

With great love hast Thou led us, O our God, and with great pity hast Thou helped us. Because our fathers believed and trusted in Thee, hast Thou taught them the laws of lfe, and shown them the way of right. We pray Thee, O Father, to give us knowledge that we may understand and do all the teachings of Thy laws. Make us obey Thy commandments and fill our hearts with love for Thee. In Thee we put our trust; we are thankful for Thy help; for by Thee alone can we be forgiven;

(Congregation standing.)

Minister:

בָּרְכוּ אֶת יְיָ הַמְבֹרָךְ:

Congregation:

בָּרוּךְ יְיָ הַמְבֹרָךְ לְעוֹלָם וָעֶד:

(Congregation sitting.)

Minister:

בָּרוּךְ אַתָּה יְיָ אֱלֹהֵינוּ מֶלֶךְ הָעוֹלָם. יוֹצֵר אוֹר
וּבוֹרֵא חֹשֶׁךְ. עֹשֶׂה שָׁלוֹם וּבוֹרֵא אֶת הַכֹּל:
הַמֵּאִיר לָאָרֶץ וְלַדָּרִים עָלֶיהָ בְּרַחֲמִים. וּבְטוּבוֹ
מְחַדֵּשׁ בְּכָל־יוֹם תָּמִיד מַעֲשֵׂה־בְרֵאשִׁית: מָה רַבּוּ
מַעֲשֶׂיךָ יְיָ. כֻּלָּם בְּחָכְמָה עָשִׂיתָ. מָלְאָה הָאָרֶץ
קִנְיָנֶךָ: תִּתְבָּרַךְ יְיָ אֱלֹהֵינוּ עַל־שֶׁבַח מַעֲשֵׂה יָדֶיךָ.
וְעַל־מְאוֹרֵי־אוֹר שֶׁעָשִׂיתָ יְפָאֲרוּךָ סֶּלָה: בָּרוּךְ אַתָּה
יְיָ יוֹצֵר הַמְּאוֹרוֹת:
אַהֲבָה רַבָּה אֲהַבְתָּנוּ יְיָ אֱלֹהֵינוּ. חֶמְלָה גְדוֹלָה
וִיתֵרָה חָמַלְתָּ עָלֵינוּ: אָבִינוּ מַלְכֵּנוּ. בַּעֲבוּר
אֲבוֹתֵינוּ שֶׁבָּטְחוּ בְךָ וַתְּלַמְּדֵם חֻקֵּי חַיִּים. כֵּן
תְּחָנֵּנוּ וּתְלַמְּדֵנוּ: הָאֵר עֵינֵינוּ בְּתוֹרָתֶךָ. וְדַבֵּק לִבֵּנוּ
בְּמִצְוֹתֶיךָ. וְיַחֵד לְבָבֵנוּ לְאַהֲבָה וּלְיִרְאָה שְׁמֶךָ. וְלֹא
נֵבוֹשׁ לְעוֹלָם וָעֶד: כִּי בְשֵׁם קָדְשְׁךָ בָּטָחְנוּ. נָגִילָה
וְנִשְׂמְחָה בִּישׁוּעָתֶךָ. כִּי אֵל פּוֹעֵל יְשׁוּעוֹת אָתָּה.

therefore we joyfully lift up our voices and praise Thy name. We bless Thee, O God, who hast shown all Israel Thy truth.

(Congregation standing.)

Minister and Congregation:

Hear, O Israel, the Lord our God, the Lord is One. Praised be His glorious name forever and ever.

(Congregation sitting.)

Minister:

THOU shalt love the Lord, Thy God, with all thy heart, with all thy soul, and with all thy might. And these words, which I command thee this day, shall be in thy heart. Thou shalt teach them carefully unto thy children, and shalt speak of them when thou sittest in thy house, when thou walkest by the way, when thou liest down, and when thou risest up. Bind them as a sign upon thy hand, and let them be as frontlets between thine eyes. Write them upon the doorposts of thy house and upon thy gates.

To the end that ye may remember and do all my commandments and be holy unto your God. I am the Lord your God.

Responsive Reading:

Minister.

THOU hast always taught us the truth through thy teachers and law-givers.

Congregation.

Thou art the living God, Thy words bring life and light to our hearts.

וּבָנוּ בָחַרְתָּ וְקֵרַבְתָּנוּ לְשִׁמְךָ הַגָּדוֹל סֶלָה בֶּאֱמֶת ׃
לְהוֹדוֹת לְךָ וּלְיַחֶדְךָ בְּאַהֲבָה ׃ בָּרוּךְ אַתָּה יְיָ
הַבּוֹחֵר בְּעַמּוֹ יִשְׂרָאֵל בְּאַהֲבָה ׃

(Congregation standing.)

Minister and Congregation:

שְׁמַע יִשְׂרָאֵל יְהוָֹה אֱלֹהֵינוּ יְהוָֹה אֶחָד ׃
בָּרוּךְ שֵׁם כְּבוֹד מַלְכוּתוֹ לְעוֹלָם וָעֶד ׃

(Congregation sitting.)

Minister:

וְאָהַבְתָּ אֵת יְיָ אֱלֹהֶיךָ בְּכָל־לְבָבְךָ וּבְכָל־נַפְשְׁךָ
וּבְכָל־מְאֹדֶךָ ׃ וְהָיוּ הַדְּבָרִים הָאֵלֶּה אֲשֶׁר אָנֹכִי
מְצַוְּךָ הַיּוֹם עַל־לְבָבֶךָ ׃ וְשִׁנַּנְתָּם לְבָנֶיךָ וְדִבַּרְתָּ
בָּם ׃ בְּשִׁבְתְּךָ בְּבֵיתֶךָ וּבְלֶכְתְּךָ בַדֶּרֶךְ וּבְשָׁכְבְּךָ
וּבְקוּמֶךָ ׃ וּקְשַׁרְתָּם לְאוֹת עַל־יָדֶךָ ׃ וְהָיוּ לְטֹטָפֹת
בֵּין עֵינֶיךָ ׃ וּכְתַבְתָּם עַל־מְזֻזוֹת בֵּיתֶךָ וּבִשְׁעָרֶיךָ ׃
לְמַעַן תִּזְכְּרוּ וַעֲשִׂיתֶם אֶת־כָּל־מִצְוֹתָי וִהְיִיתֶם
קְדוֹשִׁים לֵאלֹהֵיכֶם ׃ אֲנִי יְיָ אֱלֹהֵיכֶם ׃

Responsive Reading:

אֱמֶת ׃ אֱלֹהֵי עוֹלָם מַלְכֵּנוּ ׃ צוּר יַעֲקֹב מָגֵן יִשְׁעֵנוּ ׃
לְדוֹר וָדוֹר הוּא קַיָּם וּשְׁמוֹ קַיָּם ׃ וּמַלְכוּתוֹ
וֶאֱמוּנָתוֹ לָעַד קַיָּמֶת ׃

Thou makest us strong and givest us hope for Thy forgiveness; Thy goodness and Thy truth live for ever.

Thou hast been the help of our fathers in time of trouble; and art our help for all times.

Thou art the first and the last, and besides Thee there is no helper.

As Thou hast saved Israel so wilt Thou send Thy help to all who are in trouble.

May Thy love come to all Thy children, and Thy truth unite them like brothers.

May the good of all nations rejoice in Thy power.

O God, who art our helper and our hope, we praise Thy name.

Congregation:

Who is like Thee, O God, among the great? Who is like Thee in holiness, working wonders?

God lives forever and ever.

Minister:

O God of Israel, be pleased to save those that are in trouble, and help those that are unhappy. Praise be unto Thee, our God, the holy One of Israel.

Congregation:—Amen.

יִדְבָרָיו חָיִּים וְקַיָּמִים. נָאֱמָנִים וְנֶחֱמָדִים לָעַד
וּלְעוֹלְמֵי עוֹלָמִים:

אֱמֶת. שָׁאַתָּה הוּא יְיָ אֱלֹהֵינוּ. צוּר יְשׁוּעָתֵנוּ.
פּוֹדֵנוּ וּמַצִּילֵנוּ. מֵעוֹלָם שְׁמֶךָ. אֵין אֱלֹהִים זוּלָתֶךָ:

אַתָּה הוּא רִאשׁוֹן וְאַתָּה הוּא אַחֲרוֹן. וּמִבַּלְעָדֶיךָ
אֵין לָנוּ מֶלֶךְ גּוֹאֵל וּמוֹשִׁיעַ:

מִמִּצְרַיִם גְּאַלְתָּנוּ יְיָ אֱלֹהֵינוּ. וּמִבֵּית עֲבָדִים
פְּדִיתָנוּ:

עַל זֹאת שִׁבְּחוּ אֲהוּבִים וְרוֹמְמוּ אֵל:

Congregation:

מִי־כָמֹכָה בָּאֵלִים יְיָ. מִי כָּמֹכָה נֶאְדָּר בַּקֹּדֶשׁ
נוֹרָא תְהִלֹּת עֹשֵׂה־פֶלֶא:

Minister:

מַלְכוּתְךָ רָאוּ בָנֶיךָ. זֶה אֵלִי עָנוּ וְאָמְרוּ:

Congregation:

יְיָ יִמְלֹךְ לְעֹלָם וָעֶד:

Minister:

צוּר יִשְׂרָאֵל. קוּמָה בְּעֶזְרַת יִשְׂרָאֵל. גֹּאֲלֵנוּ יְיָ
צְבָאוֹת שְׁמוֹ. קְדוֹשׁ יִשְׂרָאֵל. בָּרוּךְ אַתָּה יְיָ גָּאַל
יִשְׂרָאֵל:

Congregation:—Amen.

Minister:

PRAISE be to Thee, O our God, God of our fa- thers Abraham, Isaac and Jacob, the great, mighty, and most high God. Thou showest loving-kindness to all Thy creatures; Thou rememberest the goodness of the fathers, and Thou sendest help to their children for the sake of Thy name. Thou art our helper and protector. Praise be to Thee, O God, father of Abraham.

Thou art mighty, O God, Thine is the power to save. In Thy kindness Thou helpest the living, holdest up the falling, healest the sick. Who is like Thee, Almighty, giver of life and death, and happiness. Praise be to Thee, O God, who hast given us life.

(Congregation standing.)

We bless Thy name on earth, even as it is blessed in heaven; and with the Rabbis we say in deep love:

Congregation:

Holy, holy, holy is the name of God, the whole earth is full of His goodness.

Minister :

בָּרוּךְ אַתָּה יְיָ אֱלֹהֵינוּ וֵאלֹהֵי אֲבוֹתֵינוּ. אֱלֹהֵי
אַבְרָהָם אֱלֹהֵי יִצְחָק וֵאלֹהֵי יַעֲקֹב. הָאֵל הַגָּדוֹל
הַגִּבּוֹר וְהַנּוֹרָא. אֵל עֶלְיוֹן. גּוֹמֵל חֲסָדִים טוֹבִים.
וְקֹנֵה הַכֹּל וְזוֹכֵר חַסְדֵי אָבוֹת. וּמֵבִיא גְאֻלָּה לִבְנֵי
בְנֵיהֶם. לְמַעַן שְׁמוֹ בְּאַהֲבָה: מֶלֶךְ עוֹזֵר וּמוֹשִׁיעַ
וּמָגֵן. בָּרוּךְ אַתָּה יְיָ מָגֵן אַבְרָהָם:

אַתָּה גִבּוֹר לְעוֹלָם אֲדֹנָי. רַב לְהוֹשִׁיעַ. מְכַלְכֵּל
חַיִּים בְּחֶסֶד. מְחַיֶּה הַכֹּל בְּרַחֲמִים רַבִּים. סוֹמֵךְ
נוֹפְלִים וְרוֹפֵא חוֹלִים וּמַתִּיר אֲסוּרִים. וּמְקַיֵּם אֱמוּנָתוֹ
לִישֵׁנֵי עָפָר. מִי כָמוֹךְ בַּעַל גְּבוּרוֹת. וּמִי דוֹמֶה־לָּךְ.
מֶלֶךְ מֵמִית וּמְחַיֶּה וּמַצְמִיחַ יְשׁוּעָה: בָּרוּךְ אַתָּה יְיָ
נָטַע בְּתוֹכֵנוּ חַיֵּי עוֹלָם:

(Congregation standing.)

נְקַדֵּשׁ אֶת שִׁמְךָ בָּעוֹלָם. כְּשֵׁם שֶׁמַּקְדִּישִׁים
אוֹתוֹ בִּשְׁמֵי מָרוֹם. כַּכָּתוּב עַל־יַד נְבִיאֶךָ. וְקָרָא
זֶה אֶל־זֶה וְאָמַר:

Congregation :

קָדוֹשׁ קָדוֹשׁ קָדוֹשׁ יְיָ צְבָאוֹת. מְלֹא כָל־הָאָרֶץ
כְּבוֹדוֹ:

Minister:

God our strength, God our Lord, how great is Thy name in all the earth.

Congregation:

In all places and countries is Thy name honored.

Minister:

Our God is One; He is our Father; He is our King; He is our Helper; and in His goodness He will answer our prayers before all the living.

Congregation:

God will live forever, thy God, O Zion, until the end of time.—Hallelujah!

(Congregation sitting.)

Minister:

DURING our whole life shall we speak of Thy greatness and throughout all ages praise Thy holiness; we shall always praise Thy name.

Grant, O God, that our rest on this day may be pleasing to Thee. Teach us to be satisfied with all Thou hast given us and thankful for all Thy blessings. Make our hearts pure that we may obey Thee in truth. O help us to keep the Sabbath as Israel's day through all times, that it may always bring rest and joy, peace and comfort to the homes of our people, and through it Thy name be blessed in all the earth.

Minister:

אַדִּיר אַדִּירֵנוּ יְיָ אֲדוֹנֵנוּ מָה־אַדִּיר שִׁמְךָ בְּכָל
הָאָרֶץ:

Congregation:

בָּרוּךְ כְּבוֹד יְיָ מִמְּקוֹמוֹ:

Minister:

אֶחָד הוּא אֱלֹהֵינוּ. הוּא אָבִינוּ. הוּא מַלְכֵּנוּ. הוּא
מוֹשִׁיעֵנוּ: וְהוּא יַשְׁמִיעֵנוּ בְּרַחֲמָיו לְעֵינֵי כָּל־חָי:

Congregation:

יִמְלֹךְ יְיָ לְעוֹלָם אֱלֹהַיִךְ צִיּוֹן לְדוֹר וָדוֹר הַלְלוּיָה:

(Congregation sitting.)

Minister:

לְדוֹר וָדוֹר נַגִּיד גָּדְלֶךָ. וּלְנֵצַח נְצָחִים קְדֻשָּׁתְךָ
נַקְדִּישׁ. וְשִׁבְחֲךָ אֱלֹהֵינוּ מִפִּינוּ לֹא יָמוּשׁ לְעוֹלָם
וָעֶד. בָּרוּךְ אַתָּה יְיָ הָאֵל הַקָּדוֹשׁ:

אֱלֹהֵינוּ וֵאלֹהֵי אֲבוֹתֵינוּ. רְצֵה בִמְנוּחָתֵנוּ. קַדְּשֵׁנוּ
בְּמִצְוֹתֶיךָ וְתֵן חֶלְקֵנוּ בְּתוֹרָתֶךָ. שַׂבְּעֵנוּ מִטּוּבֶךָ
וְשַׂמְּחֵנוּ בִּישׁוּעָתֶךָ. וְטַהֵר לִבֵּנוּ לְעָבְדְּךָ בֶּאֱמֶת.
וְהַנְחִילֵנוּ יְיָ אֱלֹהֵינוּ בְּאַהֲבָה וּבְרָצוֹן שַׁבַּת קָדְשֶׁךָ.
וְיָנוּחוּ בָהּ יִשְׂרָאֵל מְקַדְּשֵׁי שְׁמֶךָ. בָּרוּךְ אַתָּה יְיָ
מְקַדֵּשׁ הַשַּׁבָּת:

(Psalm xxiii.)

Minister:

THE Lord is my shepherd, I shall not want. He makes me lie down in green fields; He leads me beside still waters; He heals my soul; and leads me in the path of right for His name's sake. Yes, though I walk through the valley of the shadow of death, I fear no harm; Thy rod and Thy staff, O Lord, they will comfort me. Thou prepares a table for me in the sight of my enemies; Thou bathest my head with oil; my cup of joy runs over. Surely, goodness and kindness shall follow me all the days of my life; and I shall live in the house of God at all times.

Responsive Reading:

Minister.

I WILL lift up my eyes unto the hills, from where comes my help.

Congregation.

My help comes from God, the Maker of heaven and earth.

He will not allow my foot to be moved: He that keeps me will not slumber.

For, He that keeps Israel never slumbers nor sleeps.

The Lord is my keeper.

The sun shall not hurt me by day, nor the moon by night.

The Lord shall keep me from all wrong: He shall save my soul.

The Lord shall watch my going out and my coming in, from this time on, and for ever.

Lift up your eyes on high and see who has created these things, and who brings out all the stars.

The great God, the Creator of the earth, who never sleeps.

Pray to God He shall keep you; He will not allow those who pray to Him to fall.

Minister:

(Psalm xv.)

L ORD, who shall stay in Thy temple? who shall live in Thy holy hill? He who is honest, and works good, and always speaks the truth in his heart. He who never lies with his tongue, nor does wrong to others, nor talks against his neighbor. He who helps others to his own harm. He who does these things shall always be blessed.

Minister:

G IVE us peace, Thy most precious gift, O God, for Thou alone can give peace, and help Israel to be a messenger of peace to the people of the earth. Bless our country that it may always be at peace with all nations. May contentment come to all of us, health and happiness to our homes. Help us to be friends with all we meet, and to love them as our brothers. Plant good in every one of us and may the love of Thy name bless every home and every heart. Praise be to God, Giver of peace.

Congregation:—Amen.

(To be read in silence.)

אלהי נצור

O GOD, keep my tongue from bad and my lips from speaking what is not true. Be with me when grief comes to me, and comfort me when trouble makes me sad. Give peace to my mind, and strength to my heart and perfect trust in Thee. Help me to be strong when troubles come, and to be brave when others wrong me, that I may easily forgive them. Lead me by Thy help, and let me always find rest in Thee, who art my strength and my hope. Amen.

Congregation:

May the words of my mouth and the prayers of my heart be pleasing to Thee, O God, my strength and my hope.

Silent Prayers for Special Occasions.

GENERAL THANKSGIVING.

FATHER in heaven, I thank Thee for all Thy kindness to me and to my family during the past week. Every day showed me new signs of Thy love, and often I have felt that I am not worth so much goodness. If I look back upon the week, and think of all I did, I must confess that I did not live as near to Thee as I ought, nor have I done all the good I might have done. Yet, Thou knowest how much I wish to reach up higher in the perfect way, and how sorry I feel for my failings. Help me, O God, that on the next Sabbath I may have less and less cause for blame, and Thy teachings may always grow in my heart.

I pray for the life and health of all my dear family, for all who worship with me now, but especially for the sick and suffering in our midst, that Thou mayest send them comfort and help. If troubles should come to me or mine, may they find our hearts so full of faith and love that we shall never doubt Thy goodness or Thy wisdom, but shall be satisfied with Thy will and be patient, and praise Thee all the days of our lives. Amen.

THANKSGIVING FOR JOYFUL OCCASIONS.

THOU, O God, hast always been good to me, and hast often sent me joys, even when I did not deserve them. For all Thy goodness I thank Thee. And for the new happiness that has come to me (and my household) my heart is filled with thanks. Let me not grow proud because of my success, but let me enjoy Thy blessings with thanks and prayers. Do not let me forget that the best thank-offering is to bring light and joy to those that live in darkness and troubles, to give bread to the hungry, and to comfort the broken-hearted. May I, by doing what is pleasing to Thee, continue to find favor in Thy sight. Amen.

THANKSGIVING AFTER SICKNESS.

O MY God, Father of all good, I come into Thy presence to speak my thanks for the wonderful recovery from sickness.

Thy care has watched over me since childhood's days; Thou hast kept me from want; Thou hast raised me from the bed of sickness; and, often when I needed help Thou hast lifted me up and brought me to a safe place. And lately, O my God, when I was suffering pain, when my strength was gone and my soul became weak, Thou didst not let me die; Thou hast saved me, and kept me in the land of the living that I may still enjoy the sweet companionship of my beloved ones.

Therefore, with great joy and with all my soul I offer Thee my thanks. Help me so to use my strength that my life may be a blessing to others. Amen.

SILENT PRAYERS

PRAYER IN TIMES OF TROUBLE.

WISE Ruler of our lives, with a heavy heart I come before Thee in this hour of prayer; with great sadness do I seek Thee. Thou hast sent me trouble and tried me with sorrow. Mine are days of suffering and nights of weeping. I bow beneath Thy punishment and try to be satisfied. For what am I, a child of earth, that I should complain against Thy great wisdom? I know that Thy will, though hard to bear, is meant for good and not for bad. In the darkness around me, I look to Thee for light. Let me not look in vain for Thy loving arm. Comfort me, as Thou alone canst, and help me until Thou changest my mourning into joy. Let me not complain at Thy punishment, O Lord, neither be tired of Thy correction, but may my present troubles make me free from sins, correct my faults, and give me new strength to do Thy will with a perfect heart. Amen.

Minister:

O GOD bless our religion and bless all Jews who worship in thy Temples. Have pity on us and all Israel. Keep us from sickness, from trouble and from war. Keep us from hating other people or from wishing to harm them. Allow us to enjoy our work and our home-life in peace.

Congregation:

May it please our God to hear our prayer.

Minister:

Bless our children, O God, and help us to teach them that they should always love the good, and hate sin, and love and honor Thy name. May they learn Judaism and always follow its teachings and truths.

Congregation:

Our Father, God, hear our prayer and bless us.

Minister:

Bless our parents, who have done so much for us, to make us good men and women. Keep them well and strong, and help them to pass into old age in perfect happiness and health. Let us prove by our love how much we thank them for all their kindness and unselfishness, and, by our acts, how much we have learned from their teachings.

Congregation:

Hear our prayer and help us to do the right, O
   God.

Minister:

Bless all men and women who work for the good
of others, and who try to help those who are in
trouble; who give food to the hungry; clothes to
the poor; and find homes for those without friends.
Help them to carry out their good deeds, and bless
them with success.

Congregation:

May it please thee to hear our prayer.

Amen.

———————

Silent Prayer:

O GOD who art so strong that all trust in Thee, my heart is filled with thanks for the many blessings Thou gavest me. With a father's care Thou rememberest me every day and every hour. Thou hast given me reason to know the difference between right and wrong, with a mind to choose between good and bad. Thou hast opened my eyes that I may see the wonders of Thy work and, above the things of the earth, to look for Thee, O God, who are near to the hearts of the low.

Teach me, O Lord, to obey Thy will, to be satisfied with what Thou hast given me, and to share Thy gifts with those who need my help. Lead me, O Father, with Thy good advice, and keep in Thy care the lives of those dear to me. Protect my home; may peace and happiness remain in it, and love unite all who live under its roof. And when Thou sendest pain and sorrows, O give me strength to bear them patiently, and courage to trust in Thy help. Watch my going out and coming in, now and always. Amen.

Congregation:

May the words of my mouth and the thoughts in my heart be pleasing to Thee, O Lord, my strength and my helper.

Responsive Reading:

Minister.

O LORD, how many are Thy works; in wisdom hast Thou made them all; the earth is full of the riches of Thy goodness.

Congregation.

From the rising of the sun, until the going down thereof, the name of the Lord is praised.
With God are wisdom and strength.
The heavens were made by God, the earth also and all that is in it.
He made the great lights, the sun to rule by day, the moon and the stars to rule by night.
He spoke and they were made, He gave a law they cannot break.
He covers the heavens with clouds and prepares rain for the earth.
He causes grass to grow for cattle, and herbs for the use of man.
He brings forth food from the earth; wine also to please the heart of man.
Man goes out to his work from morning until the evening.
The great God has made the beginning of the world; He has placed the corner-stone of it.
The way of the Lord is perfect, His word is tried, His teachings stand forever.
The Lord lives. Blessed be the God of Israel.

Minister:

ALL you who mourn the death of loved ones, and, at this hour, remember the goodness, the hope and the sweet companionship that has passed away with them, listen to the word of comfort spoken to you in the name of your God. Only the body has died and has been laid in the grave. The spirit lives and will live on always in the land of peace and perfect happiness. But in this life, the loved ones live on in our memories. Every act of goodness they did, every true and beautiful word they spoke, is treasured up and helps us to good acts by which we honor the dead:

And when you ask in your trouble: Whence shall come my help and my comfort? then, in the belief of our religion, answer: "My help comes from God," who will be with me, and not leave me in my grief. He will give me strength to bear my troubles. All souls are His, and no power can take them out of His hands. Come, then, and in the midst of friends rise, and bless the name of God.

(The mourners standing and speaking with the Minister.)

BLESSED and honored be the name of God throughout the world which He has created, and which He governs according to His righteous will. Just is He in all His ways and wise are all His doings. May His name be loved, and His will be done in all the earth.

Congregation:

Blessed be the Lord of life and the Judge of right for evermore.

Minister:

To the dead whom we now remember, may peace and happiness be granted in the world to which they have gone. There may they find forgiveness before the Lord of heaven and earth. May their souls find joy in that great good which God has laid up for those that love Him, and may their memory be a blessing unto those they have left behind.

Congregation:

Amen.

Minister:

May the Father of peace send peace to all troubled souls, and comfort all the sorrowing among us.

Congregation:

Amen.

(The mourners standing and speaking with the Minister.)

יִתְגַּדַּל וְיִתְקַדַּשׁ שְׁמֵהּ רַבָּא. בְּעָלְמָא דִי־בְרָא
כִרְעוּתֵהּ. וְיַמְלִיךְ מַלְכוּתֵהּ. בְּחַיֵּיכוֹן וּבְיוֹמֵיכוֹן וּבְחַיֵּי
דְכָל בֵּית יִשְׂרָאֵל. בַּעֲגָלָא וּבִזְמַן קָרִיב. וְאִמְרוּ
אָמֵן:

Congregation :

יְהֵא שְׁמֵהּ רַבָּא מְבָרַךְ. לְעָלַם וּלְעָלְמֵי עָלְמַיָּא:

Minister :

יִתְבָּרַךְ וְיִשְׁתַּבַּח וְיִתְפָּאַר וְיִתְרוֹמַם וְיִתְנַשֵּׂא
וְיִתְהַדָּר וְיִתְעַלֶּה וְיִתְהַלָּל שְׁמֵהּ דְּקוּדְשָׁא. בְּרִיךְ
הוּא. לְעֵלָּא מִן כָּל בִּרְכָתָא וְשִׁירָתָא. תֻּשְׁבְּחָתָא
וְנֶחָמָתָא. דַּאֲמִירָן בְּעָלְמָא. וְאִמְרוּ אָמֵן:

עַל יִשְׂרָאֵל וְעַל צַדִּיקַיָּא. וְעַל־כָּל־מַן דְּאִתְפְּטַר
מִן עָלְמָא הָדֵין כִּרְעוּתֵהּ דֶּאֱלָהָא. יְהֵא לְהוֹן שְׁלָמָא
רַבָּא וְחוּלָקָא טָבָא לְחַיֵּי עָלְמָא דְּאָתֵי. וְחִסְדָּא
וְרַחֲמֵי מִן־קֳדָם מָרֵא שְׁמַיָּא וְאַרְעָא. וְאִמְרוּ אָמֵן:

יְהֵא שְׁלָמָא רַבָּא מִן־שְׁמַיָּא וְחַיִּים. עָלֵינוּ וְעַל־כָּל־
יִשְׂרָאֵל. וְאִמְרוּ אָמֵן:

עֹשֶׂה שָׁלוֹם בִּמְרוֹמָיו. הוּא יַעֲשֶׂה שָׁלוֹם עָלֵינוּ
וְעַל כָּל יִשְׂרָאֵל. וְאִמְרוּ אָמֵן:

CLOSING HYMN.

WHO is like Thee, O all-loving Lord?
　Who dare Thy praise and glory share?
Who is in heaven, Most High, like Thee adored?
Who can on earth with Thee compare?
Thou art the One true God alone,
And firmly founded is Thy throne.

Thy tender love embraces all mankind,
As children all by Thee are blest;
Repentant sinners with Thee mercy find,
Thy hand upholdeth the opprest;
All worlds attest Thy power sublime,
Thy glory shines in every clime.

And to Thy might and love is joined in Thee
The highest wisdom's living spring;
Whate'er to us is deepest mystery,
Is clean to Thee, our Lord and King.
O God of wisdom, love and might,
We worship Thee, Eternal Light.

BENEDICTION.

CLOSING HYMN.

אֵין כֵּאלֹהֵינוּ ‧ אֵין כַּאדוֹנֵינוּ ‧

אֵין כְּמַלְכֵּנוּ ‧ אֵין כְּמוֹשִׁיעֵנוּ :

מִי כֵאלֹהֵינוּ ‧ מִי כַאדוֹנֵינוּ ‧

מִי כְמַלְכֵּנוּ ‧ מִי כְמוֹשִׁיעֵנוּ :

נוֹדֶה לֵאלֹהֵינוּ ‧ נוֹדֶה לַאדוֹנֵינוּ ‧

נוֹדֶה לְמַלְכֵּנוּ ‧ נוֹדֶה לְמוֹשִׁיעֵנוּ :

בָּרוּךְ אֱלֹהֵינוּ ‧ בָּרוּךְ אֲדוֹנֵינוּ ‧

בָּרוּךְ מַלְכֵּנוּ ‧ בָּרוּךְ מוֹשִׁיעֵנוּ :

אַתָּה הוּא אֱלֹהֵינוּ ‧ אַתָּה הוּא אֲדוֹנֵינוּ

אַתָּה הוּא מַלְכֵּנוּ ‧ אַתָּה הוּא מוֹשִׁיעֵנוּ

BENEDICTION.

BENEDICTION.

———

Minister:

OUR God, may Thy blessing rest upon us, according to the gracious promise of Thy word:

יְבָרֶכְךָ יְיָ וְיִשְׁמְרֶךָ:

May the Lord bless thee and keep thee!

Congregation:—Amen.

יָאֵר יְיָ פָּנָיו אֵלֶיךָ וִיחֻנֶּךָ:

May the Lord let His countenance shine upon thee and be gracious unto thee!

Congregation:—Amen.

יִשָּׂא יְיָ פָּנָיו אֵלֶיךָ וְיָשֵׂם לְךָ שָׁלוֹם:

May the Lord lift up His countenance upon thee and give thee peace!

Congregation:—Amen.

————